the smart girl's guide to college

The Smart Girl's

GUIDE TO COLLEGE

A Serious Book
Written by
Women in College to
Help You Make
the Perfect College Choice

Edited by Cristina Page

The Noonday Press
A division of Farrar, Straus and Giroux
New York

The Noonday Press
A division of Farrar, Straus and Giroux
19 Union Square West, New York 10003

Copyright © 1997 by Cristina Page
All rights reserved
Distributed in Canada by Douglas & McIntyre Ltd.
Printed in the United States of America
Designed by Liney Li
First edition, 1997

Library of Congress Cataloging-in-Publication Data
The smart girl's guide to college : a serious book written by women in
college to help you make the perfect college choice / edited by
Cristina Page. — 1st ed.
      p.   cm.
   ISBN 0-374-52514-5 (paper : alk. paper)
   1. Women—Education (Higher)—Social aspects—United States.
2. College choice—United States.   3. College student orientation—
United States.   4. Women college students—United States—Conduct
of life.   5. Universities and colleges—United States—Sociological
aspects.   I. Page, Cristina, 1970–   .
LC1757.S63   1997   97-12833
378.1'9822—dc21

Sources for endpaper time line include the following: Irene M. Franck and
David M. Brownstone, Women's World: A Time Line of Women in
History (New York: Harper Perennial, 1995). Sue Heinemann, Timelines
of American Women's History (New York: Berkley Publishing Group/
A Perigee Book, 1996). Mabel Newcomer, A Century of Higher
Education for American Women (New York: Harper & Brothers,
1959)
Information for Title IX section taken from the following: Kathryn M. Reith,
Playing Fair: A Guide to Title IX in High School and College Sports
(East Meadow: The Women's Sports Foundation, 1994)
Time line and interior illustrations copyright © 1997 by Jeffrey Fulvimari

to steve

contents

Three: The Social Scene

Four: Living, Playing, Working, Learning

Five: In the Know

the smart girl's guide to college

introduction

I know what you're going through. I remember a scene from my high school years which is probably similar to something you are experiencing now or will very soon. It's my parents perched in the front seat of our Nissan Maxima cruising at legal speed down I-95, my father at the wheel. Something seriously embarrassing, like "Jesus Christ Superstar," was playing on the tape deck. My mother flipped through the catalogue of the college to which we were headed. I sat in the back seat, trying to convince them to play the Beastie Boys tape I brought along, and, all-in-all, was being the difficult child I had spent fifteen years perfecting. This was my family in search of my second home—college.

My mother had started my college search before I did— long before. She says that, when I was still a glimmer in her eye, she had a picture of me in mind. It was of a curly-haired, quiet girl who wore glasses and read voraciously. The kind made for a small, all-women's, very academic college which had equestrian programs and ballet requirements, and was attended by governors' daughters. That was my mother's dream. Instead, I was born with straight hair; grew up loud and with perfect vision; needed to be forced to do homework; and had just about enough of the all-women's thing at the all-girls' high school. But while we drove down south, my mother still had one part of that dream alive, the college part, and if it was to die—it was gonna die hard.

Then there was the Catholic high school college counselor—the ying to my mother's yang. Sister Marie was really pushing the Catholic college route. After all, she had connections in "high places," and it would be easier for me to get in. She showed me graphs and charts of past graduates and the colleges they went to—emphasizing that not many had chosen to go to the secular ones I had as my top choices. She explained that most of my classmates were Catholic college-bound; therefore, I was already friends with the type of women who go to these colleges. It was a place where I would fit in, a place where I could continue my Catholic education. That was my college counselor's plan.

Day and night, I spent my sophomore year listening to other people's ideas of what was best for me. I remember the frustration of not being able to speak for myself, of not knowing what I wanted in a college, because I had no idea what college really was. Most of the guidebooks just provided numbers. The only one that came close to any insight was Lisa Birnbach's like really superficial college guide—which was sort of a fun read, but nothing I wanted to bet four years on. So, as we drove to and from prospective schools, and as I nodded politely while tour guides gave scripted answers to all my difficult and sometimes controversial questions, I was resigned to let the people who knew more move me like a chess piece from high school into college.

Once I got to college and became used to my surroundings, I realized that there are so many things that affect your happiness, so many questions I should have asked but didn't. I didn't know to. Apparently, many people don't. Presently, one out of four students drops out of college, or transfers to another, before sophomore year. This suggests that many students are selecting colleges that aren't right for them—a situation that could have been avoided had they looked more closely at their colleges choices. Many of the things that my friends and I loved or hated about college had to do with the fact that we were *women* in college. Being in a sorority is different from being in a fraternity; going to a college in a city presents issues for women that it doesn't for men; some schools have men's sports programs that rock while their women's sports programs barely exist; taking a women's-studies class effects women and men differently. College is not better or worse for men or women, it is simply different.

As a girl, you are heading off to college at a very interesting time in history. Women are now the majority of college students, 55 percent. Today, in all racial groups, more women are attending college than men. By the year 2005, it is expected that 1.6 million more women will be in college than men. Today, the most popular major for women is business management. It should then come as no surprise that studies by psychologists have found that women in college today are more assertive, action-oriented, and goal-driven than they were twenty years ago. Something the researchers oddly term "more masculine."

And even though your generation of women is thought of as "more masculine," you will differ from your male counterparts in many ways. You are more likely to earn better grades than the guys in your classes, and less likely to cheat on a test to get them. You are more likely to go to graduate school than a man, and you're also more likely to be awarded the prestigious Rhodes scholarship. If you're an athlete, you are more likely to graduate on time than are your male counterparts, 69 percent and 53 percent, respectively. You are more likely to study abroad than men are (63 percent of students studying abroad are women). And because there are now more all-women's colleges than all-men's colleges, for the first time in history you have more college choices than men do.

How colleges differ from one another will figure prominently in your decision-making. There are the general differences, like size, location, reputation, which all define a campus environment. However, there are many other important things which may seem like small details on a tour but which turn out to be characteristics that say a lot about a school. Whether the health center provides or doesn't provide birth control says something. The ratio of male to female tenured professors says something. The existence of a school-supported gay and lesbian student organization says something. The option to live in a single-sex dorm says something. When you select a college, it's up to you to decide whether you like what you hear. But, to do this, you must first understand what is being said.

The people who can best explain what it all means, and why you should care, are the people who are living it right now: women in college. They are people like you, who had the same questions about college just a few years ago and now have the answers. Only they know what it's like to go to an all-women's college today; to be a black woman at a predominately white college right now; or to have feminist views at a religious school in the late 1990s. In the following pages, they will show you, from a female perspective, the Ivy League college, the large state university, the black college, and the military academy. They'll show you the ins and outs of work-study, the pros and cons of a school close to or far from home, and what life is like at a liberal college and a conservative one. They'll take you through the coed and single-sex dorms, to the frat parties and sorority house meetings, into the large lectures and small seminars, while pointing out all the things tour guides seem to overlook. Their stories are all about what it is like to be a woman in college today. They don't have an agenda, or any reason to want you to pick one school over another. They are simply telling you the facts about all the options—giving you the information you need to make a more educated college choice.

How to Use This Book

You can use this book in many ways. You can mix and match the essays. For instance, if you're thinking about going to a large state university with a Greek system in a rural setting, you can read the essays by Laura, Katie, Keely, and Jesse to see what that would be like. Or you can read the book chapter by chapter to see what all your options are. You should know that every essay was written with you in mind, even if it doesn't seem to be. If you're white, you can learn from the experiences of Angine, who tells what it's like to be a black woman at a predominately white school. If you're heterosexual, Kelly's essay about being lesbian at an intolerant college shows how important it is to be true to yourself when choosing a school. Most important, these stories will help you judge how well a college creates an environment that is comfortable for students of many experiences and perspectives—comfortable for the people who will be your future friends, roommates, and classmates.

At the back of the book is a questionnaire that you can use to find out the important information which colleges don't include in their catalogues. The section on standardized tests fills you in on options other than the SAT, which has been found to be biased against girls. The "Your Rights" chapter explains all the laws passed to protect women in college. The resource section has valuable information about scholarships offered just for women, about women's college sports and colleges that don't require standardized tests, and on-line hookups to hundreds of campus newspapers and home pages, as well as ways to submit your applications electronically.

Choosing a college is one of the most important decisions you will ever make. The college you select will help shape your values, your ideas, your goals, and who you turn out to be. With this book, I hope to help you make the right choice by giving you all the perspectives I wish I had had when I was in your shoes.

—Cristina Page

One

Where

It's

At

urban vs. rural

*It is important to match a college environment with your
personality and expectations, especially when you're dealing
in extremes, such as a rural or urban setting. In the following essays, Catherine Moore explains cosmopolitan college life, and Katie Ford shows us the country side.*

The Concrete College

by Catherine Moore

I was well aware that life at a city university would be
different from life at the small-town college campuses I had
visited. My parents would much rather have had me go to a
university in a small town populated by students, professors'
families, and dorms with midnight curfews. While small-
town campuses surrounded by cornfields appealed to me in
some ways, the excitement and resources of the city seemed
to offer a more comprehensive education. Needless to say,
by enrolling at Loyola University in Chicago, I got more than
I had bargained for.

Tree-lined quads and rows of Greek houses were noticeably absent from the view from my dorm window. Instead, I watched the endless comings and goings of Chicagoans as they traveled the elevated train system, located across from my residence hall. Fortunately, if I strained my neck to the right, I could glimpse the beautiful blue waves of Lake Michigan lapping at the edge of our campus. This was only my first taste of the city's extremes.

I was alone and free in a city that never sleeps. If anything can be both empowering and overwhelming at the same time, this was it. What do you do and what don't you do when you have a whole city and four years to play with? Scenes of evenings at the theater, late nights in little jazz bars, days walking around archives, galleries, and museums filled my head and made me dizzy. I couldn't think of a better education. I made lists of places to go and things to do, filling my weeks with schedules of social events and cultural offerings.

Unfortunately, urban culture was not the only classroom in Chicago. It would be wonderful to let the city be my teacher, but my professors were vying for equal time. Although most diversions were only an el ride away from campus, class and term papers seemed a million miles from row 3, seat 17, at the Steppenwolf Theatre, where John Malkovich was performing. French class soon competed with Cub games; I spent time inventing convincing arguments that one more beer wouldn't affect my ability to get up at 7:30 a.m. to take my philosophy quiz.

Study time is not the only thing that is affected by the enticements of college life in an urban environment. In Chicago, cash flows like green beer on Saint Patrick's Day. Neither city life nor a college education is cheap. The combination of the two can put a strain on a student's checking account. It is difficult enough to part with $300 a semester for a pile of books (some of which you may never crack open), and city life has its price as well. Little things like dinner at something other than the greasy spoon known as the university dining hall can add up before you know it. If you're not careful, urban living can suck your Stafford Loan dry.

Then there are the dangers of traveling, meeting odd people, passing through dangerous neighborhoods. Loyola's brochure said nothing about drug dealers on the el or panhandlers outside our student union. The admissions office couldn't have informed my classmate Ethan that his college career at Loyola would be cut short by a man with a gun who wanted Ethan's car and instead took his life. The photos of students sharing coffee in our downtown café didn't feature the man who followed my roommate home one night and stalked her all last semester.

But these are not common scenes at our college, where there had never been a murder before, so they are perhaps more jarring because our campus is generally safe. But in a university in a city, you are faced every day with the city that is your campus and home. While you are attending college to become empowered, the very institution of education can become threatening, especially to a woman when three rapes occur within one week only blocks from your residence hall and your friend gets mugged on the el as you sit across from him. Being in a city is an exciting thing, but you also have to recognize the flip side. Women can't walk alone at night, meeting new people at bars and clubs is not always safe, and your bicycle may get stolen from a locked rack. A good university, however, will prepare you for the dangers around campus. Twenty-four-hour escorts, self-defense classes,

and crime prevention and awareness have kept Loyola
students, especially women, from becoming victims.

The challenge of attending a city university comes in bal-
ancing all the temptations the city offers with the realities of
being an eighteen-year-old with a meager income and an
abundance of educational and financial responsibilities. A
little enterprise helped me create a relationship between
what I was doing in the classroom as an English major and
the sundry offerings of Chicago.

Employed by a well-known Chicago bookseller, I earned
spending money while meeting authors like Maya Angelou
and John Grisham, getting free books, making friends and
noteworthy connections. I was invited to gallery openings,
movie previews, and poetry recitals, and I hobnobbed with
National Public Radio personalities. My fellow employees
christened me into the retail book business along with all the
interesting customers, including the gentleman who carried
a briefcase of random newspaper clippings from the past fifty
years and the woman who would flip through a book and
then recite it word for word in the middle of the store.

My junior year "Theater in Chicago" class enabled me to
enjoy plays while learning about drama and receiving course
credit. Editing the school newspaper gave me the opportunity to work with an NBC producer on a local story. Three
rapes that occurred near campus in broad daylight led me to
campaign successfully for twenty-four-hour security escorts.
My clinical hours working in a local Chicago public elementary school gave me the chance to work with youngsters.

Chicago truly became a classroom for me. I became responsible, developed a work ethic, made a wealth of wonderfully interesting friends, and learned some hard realities,
as well. I learned not to wear a skirt when you might end up
dancing on a bar, that the woman sleeping under the library

air vent might need the dollar more than I need the Coke I would have bought with it, and that many of the kids I teach on Wednesday afternoons will probably never get the chance to go to college.

College in the city was not a sanctum ritual of classes on the lawn followed by common meals in the cafeteria and alternating nights of studying and beer parties, as attractive as that might sound. I've read my fair share of Shakespeare and studied enough energy and matter to construct a galaxy. And it was wonderful. But seeing *A Midsummer Night's Dream* performed by the Royal Shakespeare Company and helping my sixth-grade class learn about planets on a field trip to the Adler Planetarium cannot be replaced. The taking was, beyond a doubt, more than the giving.

Catherine Moore plans on becoming a high school teacher.

Fields of Dreams

by Katie Ford

Whitman College ships incoming freshmen boxes of Walla Walla sweet onions with recipes for ways to fry and bake and ring the onions. In August, on your way into town, onion stands dot the side of the road every half mile; you can smell them long before you can see their red-and-white paint. To the west, there are raging yellow canola farms; to the north, blue mountain ridges; and all around there is wheat. While I am at Whitman, in the small town of Walla Walla, Washington, this landscape is my frame of reference for looking at the world, and it encourages both personal reflection and social creativity.

Many students come to Whitman for the outdoor activities, which soon take over their social life. There are always stories of friends repelling off local grain silos in the middle of the night, of groups building snow caves in the Blue Mountains for shelter on a camping trip, and of picnics in the September wheatfields.

Weekend ideas need to be inventive and fresh, because town shuts down at around ten in the evening—except for the two bars nicknamed "the blue" and "the green." There are other bars, but in a small town the places most familiar are the ones with nicknames, which quickly become part of the Whitman lingo along with other timeless labels: whitties, townies, twitties, pinging, Lakum Dukum, and the red. The red is where you go when everything else is closed—it's the kind of diner that has pastries which taste like cigarettes. Students have opened their own coffee shops near campus, showing that living in the country makes students more resourceful and active, since the only Broadway we have leads to the $1.75 theater and a llama farm.

My social life has become more intimate since I've been in college—like having Stephen cook a thick pasta dish for me that he discovered in Italy, going for drives through the Columbia Gorge in Pete's blue Chevy just to get away and listen to old music, or playing cribbage with Cathy two floors down while drinking a flat rum and Coke. A lot of students have cars, which allows them to get farther off campus, but cars aren't necessary, since most things in town can be reached by bike or on foot and it's always possible to car pool.

Last fall semester I was able to take a poetry class so small that we met once a week out at the professor's house on the river. We drove the forty-five minutes to his canyon-line shack down a winding rocky road through the farmlands, knowing his house by the horse in the pasture and the winter orchard a half mile before. We sat around the wood-burning stove critiquing each other's poetry, watching the wasps occasionally crawl out of the cedar slats of the walls. When we took a break, the professor told me to go grab a bottled soda out of the river near the rock beds. I walked out past the boarded-up outhouse and the cat on the woodpile to find a few root beers among the river rocks. Only in Walla Walla, I thought.

That is a common thought and it is used both positively and negatively in such a small town. Only here do people go to the dorm's western windows to watch the sun set purple and red because of the stirred-up dust on the land; only here is a park safe and empty in midmorning, with a circle of Chinese cherry trees to sit inside. But only here is a big concert unheard of, a dance club nonexistent, and a poetry slam foreign. From what I've seen, life in the country stirs up either a strong frustration in people or a peace which hurries them to the kind of reflection that changes or solidifies one's perspective.

The campus supplements outside social life with efforts to keep us busy on the weekends with concerts in the outdoor amphitheater, late-night barn dances, and coffeehouses. The crowd is fairly diverse, even though we've all chosen a small college in a small town, with the most common trait being bare feet and an ability to recognize everybody on the grass in front of the band.

During a hike through the Blue Mountains, my friend Emily taught me that I could eat off the huckleberry bushes without dying, so we did it throughout our long walk in the hills. Sometimes being isolated, as on that day in the Blues, simplifies and slows things down. But this February, when flooding rivers boxed the town in, a lot of students felt claustrophobic, knowing that the highways were closed to Portland, Seattle, Boise—every major city in every direction. We weren't allowed to stand on bridges, some dorms were evacuated for a while, and lots of college students joined the town in sandbagging out on the river. The sense of being trapped made the campus psyche nearly close in on itself, showing that our access to cities is what frees us to enjoy the country.

Katie Ford plans to study creative writing.

far from or close to home

One of the biggest decisions of all is how much distance to put between college and home. Fifty-seven percent of students choose a school far enough away to require a phone call before a visit. What you have to decide is whether you want your parents looking for a parking space or a hotel reservation. In the following essays, Junelle Harris will show you that there is a difference between moving out and moving on, and Elena Olsen will show you what being a long-distance daughter can be like.

See You in December

by Elena Olsen

Yawning as if I had spent many mornings in the airport waiting to fly east to Philadelphia, I unzipped my sophisticatedly shabby duffel and put my *New Yorker* on top of my camera and extra change of clothes, for easy access on the plane (people would see me reading *The New Yorker* and think, "Ah, a young woman on her way to college"). I gazed out the window at the Boeing 757, hoping my brain waves would force the gate to open so the boarding could begin. I searched for the nearest restroom, I stared at my Birkenstocks, I looked everywhere but at my mother's blubbering eyes and my father's sheet-tight face. I was actually rather surprised at the loud snufflings and gushings of my mother's tears; I had expected a few bittersweet drops trickling down her otherwise beaming, proud, familiarly stoic face. You'd think it was the nineteenth century and I was going off to seek my fortune nevermore to return—which wouldn't necessarily be that heartbreaking either, since I was getting really tired of tiptoeing up the stairs every Saturday night to tell my parents that I was home, safe and sound and sober.

After a series of woeful smiles I shoved my ticket at the flight attendant, hurled a smile and wave back at my parents—perhaps too cheerleader-like in the face of their anguish. I walked down the gateway, savoring this great Going Away to College. For this long plane trip from Seattle to Philadelphia confirmed and guaranteed my ensuing independence, severing me from my parents before I even arrived at college. I was so thankful that my parents could not drive me to school, cart all my stuff up to my room, fuss about the lack of lighting and drawer space, smile suspiciously at my roommate, and take me out to dinner one last time. In choosing a college 2,800 miles across the country, I was truly originating a new and glorious student life which my parents paid for but could not monitor as they had monitored all my activities for eighteen years. My mother and I had agreed that the fact that I was ready and eager to venture far from home proved both my maturity and the effectiveness of my parents' raising of me. My hard work throughout high school now culminated in a well-deserved, triumphant journeying to "the East," that ivy-clad, leather-bound bastion of Boston accents, Harvard scholars, "old money."

Shining not with triumph but with the grime of seven hours in a poorly ventilated plane, I stood at the edge of a huge parking lot somewhere on the Bryn Mawr College campus. I had imagined some sort of welcoming committee, a liberated, happily hairy-legged sisterhood of all-knowing Bryn Mawrters waiting to greet the frosh. These Mawrters, much more helpful, and certainly more hip, than any parents could be, would proceed to whisk me to my room, assuring me through their effusive friendliness and savvy that Bryn Mawr was indeed the Perfect Place for Me. But no such welcome materialized. I stood there alone in the gray parking lot, longing for a blast of cool Pacific Northwest air in the sodden, polluted Eastern heat, and for someone to tell me where to go and remind me why this strangely silent women's college in the middle of Pennsylvania was the Perfect Place for Me. Turning, I saw a sign reading, "Bryn Mawr College Office of Public Safety." I dragged my two gargantuan suitcases and now-torn duffel into the doorway and smiled confidently at the officer behind the desk, and explained, "I'm an early-arrival freshman from the West Coast and I need to get my keys and find my dorm." The blue-uniformed woman leaned back in her chair and, barely looking up from her *Philadelphia Inquirer*, informed me, "It's too late to get your keys. We can unlock the door for you, I guess. Go ahead and I'll send someone over. It might be a while." "My dorm is Rhoads South, and I don't know exactly how to get there. And I have three bags. Can I get some help?" She snapped forward in her chair, crinkling her newspaper, pointed out the window, and said in a maternal "How-many-times-have-I-told-you-this" voice: "Rhoads South is straight across. We don't do luggage." Simultaneously mortified and indignant—all I wanted was a luggage cart, for Pete's sake!—I straggled across the huge expanse of greenness, ogling the intimidating nineteenth-century collegiate gothic architecture and trying to keep in mind the direction of the officer's pointing finger.

Over the following turbulent months of that first semester, I struggled to attain a sense of direction and "athomeness." From the weirdly old-fashioned air-raid siren which was used to alert the community's volunteer firemen and which woke me up at all hours of the night, to my feeling trapped inside Bryn Mawr's turreted, gargoyled buildings, not knowing how to find a grocery store outside this gray fortress, to my growing awareness that perhaps Bryn Mawr was not the Perfect Place for Me, life at this Eastern institution began to convince me that my high school counselor's warning of "culture shock" was not so ridiculous. I was continually reminded that going to school three thousand miles away from home meant not only that my parents could not catch me with my boyfriend or a beer at 3 a.m. but also that they could not meet my freshman-year adviser and realize how horrible she was. They could not tell me just to go to bed and not worry about finishing my homework; they could not be sitting in their favorite chairs in the living room every night, telling me how proud they were of all I was doing, and that they would find a way to fix any problems. I made almost daily phone calls home, with either bubbly stories of new acquaintances or teary tirades against the administration, who put me into an English class I hated and would not let a professor "overload" an eighteen-member class. When I felt that the administration was treating me like a second-class citizen of the Bryn Mawr community since I had gone to a public high school in a dinky little town in Washington state, my phone bill soared in one day just so I could hear my mother validate my indignation with her own huffing and puffing.

Feeling like a wispy stick figure blown by the hot breeze among the happily hairy-legged Mawrters who played cello for the Philadelphia Orchestra and knew Latin and Greek from their pre-school educations and had lived everywhere from Lesotho to Iceland, I drifted from class to the dining hall to my room in self-pitying insecurity. I was compelled to ask my mom about every decision I needed to make: which classes to take, how to confront my adviser about my concerns, whether or not to buy a rug for my room. Then, I began to realize that I was able, in this fortress of female learning, to immerse myself in *myself*: in how I, not my parents or my distinguished classmates, responded to life. Due in part to my ruinous phone bill, I decided that I did not have to ask my mom what courses would be best for me to take the second semester, nor did I have to ask her if I could visit a friend in Georgetown for the weekend. I could just jump on a train and go. Even if I skimped on my Spanish and bio reading to do so, I did not need to feel guilty when my mother worried, "Are you sure you have time for this?" since I was exploring an area of the world I had never seen, and to me that was part of my Bryn Mawr education.

For the first several weeks of school my roommate, who lived forty-five minutes away, would, after her last class on Fridays, flee home to her own bedroom and kitchen, despite brave resolutions to "stick it out." Not being able to retreat to familiarity, I mooned around alone in my room with my new Indigo Girls CD and my journal, or I went to bizarre parties where I talked for hours about the virtues of bras or Sylvia Plath. I made courageous efforts to bond with my fellow Mawrters by participating in midnight skinny-dipping excursions to a fountain behind the library, but ended up running away, neither worldly-wise nor high enough to appreciate the transcendent bliss of this experience.

I am now in the end of my spring semester, junior year, at Bryn Mawr College, and still do not feel comfortable stripping down in the middle of campus, but I am aware, perhaps more profoundly than during my first year, that the immense distance between myself and my home can be both liberating and disorienting. When I only hear about but not see my brother's tennis victories and new girlfriend, I realize that the August morning in the airport three years ago did indeed mark my going-away-never-to-return. My parents are more slowly becoming aware of the implications of sending me off and still surprise me, as they did in the airport freshman year, with their frequent "I wish you could be here" emotions. Home to me now is my dorm room with three years' worth of books, posters, pictures, wineglasses, or my friends' rooms, more familiar to me than the living room at my family's house.

At times of course I still feel lost, wandering, in need of a guiding voice, but rather than picking up the phone, I sit down on my bed and stare out the window, examining my own instincts, or I write in my journal, just as I did freshman year if my mother wasn't home when I needed to talk to her. The three thousand miles between myself and my "home" not only set me adrift but also, and with increasing frequency, enlarge and free my way of experiencing the world. I have come to see that, though I retain certain attitudes and qualities of my parents, I am living a far different life than either of my parents lived, and I have in me far different attitudes, values, and hopes than my parents do. Furthermore, I am beginning to acknowledge that these differences in both life-style and character are not necessarily grounds for rebellion or resentment, but rather for increased sensitivity in myself as well as my parents.

My major adviser, whom my mother has never met, is now the person I turn to for advice about classes and the future. In fact, after my major adviser urged me to take a poetry-writing workshop and I mentioned this to my mother in one of our weekly—not daily—phone conversations, she scoffed and then, when she realized I was serious, declared in her "Be-Sensible-Elena" voice that poets were a bunch of flakes and that a poetry workshop would not help me get into a good grad school. When I tried to convey to her my deep love for poetry, which stemmed from two classes in which I had read a good deal of it for the first time in my life, she snapped at me that I already sounded flaky and "not like the real Elena." This reaction surprised and hurt me deeply, since I was speaking from what I know, and my friends know, and my English professors know, as my "most real" self.

The life I live here, among friends, professors, and total strangers, constitutes my "home," however alien and even hostile it sometimes seems. Importantly, weekends spent with total strangers, lonely nights spent sitting on my hands to keep them from picking up the phone, parties where I listened, mute, to others' stories about their world travels, have all taught me that amid life's never-ending uprootings, I cannot, ultimately, turn to anyone but myself for direction and affirmation.

Elena Olsen spent the summer studying at the University of Trier, in Trier, Germany.

Close Encounters

by Junelle Harris

*t*hroughout college, my parents have always been there for me. Sometimes, it might seem, they've been a little too close. Like numerous other parents, they have spent countless hours and dollars offering over-the-phone counseling. Unlike many other college students, I have had the added disadvantage/advantage of house calls. At times, the short distance which allows this has truly been fortuitous: when my computer crashed days before finals week, my mother drove to my college to lend me her own computer. Other times, it has been trying. On one occasion, my father offered his own brand of help. When I found myself embroiled in a particularly sticky bureaucratic situation, my father threatened to drive over and "set those people"—the Office of Residential Life—"straight." I only narrowly succeeded in convincing him that I could handle the problem myself.

My freshman-year boyfriend was less fortunate—his parents lived five minutes' drive from our residence hall. One day, his mother dropped by and found us studying in his room. She noted his liquor-bottle collection and my usually tousled hair, and asked if we didn't think it was really better to keep the door open when we were in the room together. Periodically during the rest of the year, she would stop by, "just to see how he was doing." The next year, he ended up transferring, to put distance between himself and his parents.

Growing up in a small, conservative rural town in Idaho, I had dreamed for years of getting away to "the big city." During my junior year of high school, I pored over the hundreds of brochures that colleges all over the nation sent me. I still planned on attending college far from home, but my high school counselor gave me information from his alma mater, a small but reputable liberal-arts school in Idaho, "just in case."

I sent out applications and was accepted to a number of schools, but I couldn't decide where I wanted to go. I liked the University of Chicago, a large school in a large city several thousand miles away, for the strength of its academic reputation and the diversity of its programs and students. I liked Albertson College of Idaho, a small private liberal-arts college (under seven hundred students), for its size, student-to-teacher ratio, and location, which was relatively close to home. During my senior year, I felt overwhelmed by the "significant life decisions" that I had to make and was beginning to wonder if staying close to home might not be such a bad idea, after all. Although I had traveled extensively, I had never lived outside of Idaho. I searched for the souvenir my father purchased for me in Chicago when I was seven. It was a snow globe with a cityscape. Across the front of the buildings, a sign read CHICAGO: THE WINDY CITY. Watching the snowflakes swirl down, I thought what a cold, desolate place Chicago might be. I reasoned that by attending Albertson College I would have a chance to be on my own without being separated from all that I was familiar with. I could attend graduate school in "the big city" later.

I decided to go to Albertson. I would be close enough to return home when I needed to, but distant enough that I would not be directly on my parents' doorstep. My best friend, Cynthia, and I were among the few from our high school to go to college outside our small town, which had its own two-year religious institution. She was on her way to Bryn Mawr in Pennsylvania, some two thousand miles away. We were both excited. It wasn't until Christmas break of that first year that I began to question both our decisions.

It was December and I couldn't wait to see Cynthia. Over the course of the fall term, we had sporadically exchanged letters and phone calls. I remember the first postcard that she sent me. It had a picture of a tall clock tower (my own school had a similar tower). Cynthia told me about the diversity on her campus, assuring me that "you would love it here." I told her about the things I was doing and the new friends I had made. My campus wasn't as diverse as hers, and sometimes I did feel that I was missing out by attending a college in conservative, demographically homogeneous Idaho. There were the familiar annoyances: people still regularly stared at my mildly eccentric clothing; my friends and I listened to punk music and perused avant-garde books but didn't have much opportunity to experience either firsthand; I was quickly labeled the "campus feminist"—a designation which I was not ashamed of, but one that was not altogether complimentary in the eyes of many. But I was where I wanted, experiencing new things, more challenging classes, personal responsibility, new people, campus drinking, and different life-styles, in an environment that was comfortably familiar. Some seemingly trivial familiarities were important. Cynthia missed the mountains; I could see them every day. My parents took pains to allow me room to grow, but I knew that if I needed them I could see them every day. When I was sick, they encouraged me to come home for homemade food and care. Cynthia had to spend Thanksgiving with friends; I could invite friends who lived far away from home to spend Thanksgiving with me.

I wondered what every person wonders when meeting someone they have been separated from for a time. How has that person changed? The first change that immediately struck me was Cynthia's hair. Her pale blond hair was dyed bright orange, the result of a drunken lark. She dragged me out into the cold Idaho weather to talk while she smoked Camel Lights, a habit she had previously found "disgusting." Then there were the stories about drunken parties, her new drug experimentation and sexual activities with different men and women. Common friends had remarked that she had "gone away and gone wild." While these experiences were less foreign to me than to our other friends who attended the local religious institution, I was struck by her immersion in the "diversity" of her newfound environment. In addition, her nonchalance presumed a cool superiority; and my lack of visible change, both in environment and in manner, seemed to mark me as unadventurous and unsophisticated in her eyes. I knew that these changes in Cynthia reflected more than a change in environment, but I also knew that her new environment freed her from both the psychic and the literal constraints of being close to home. At my own school, I regularly met people who knew my parents, their friends or acquaintances. Though I have never shied away from expressing myself, both familiarity with my environment and the proximity of my parents led me to consider the consequence of my actions. I generally find this a positive thing, but I couldn't help but wonder . . .

I have continued to wonder "what if" and "what next." I am approaching the end of my junior year and am faced with many of the same "significant life decisions" I had to make at the end of high school. I attend college with many students like myself, who have decided to experience the new challenges of college life in close proximity to the comforts of home. Most, like myself, see this as an important stage of development before moving on to bigger and better things. I have also been able to observe the varied levels of success with which different people are able to make that transition.

Some become accustomed to the relative comfort and even complacency of being on home turf. I have friends who were born, raised, and will probably live and die within a fifty-mile radius. They continue to rely on their parents as a primary social outlet. After graduating from college, they have avoided taking risks which would move them out of this comfort zone. One, who aspires to be a journalist, gave up a great opportunity to work in New York. After discussing the move with his parents, teachers, and friends, he decided that, in the face of the risks involved (meeting and working with new people, having to prove himself, navigating the city), he wanted to stay on familiar ground. I, along with other friends, regretted what we saw as a lost opportunity. We took the situation as a lesson for ourselves.

Others do appreciate the need for different horizons. Another aspiring journalist friend from my college, who has lived in Idaho most of his life, recently moved to Washington, D.C. There he worked first as a waiter but has now netted a job working as a media consultant for a left-wing organization. He values the education he received, but only, he says, because he has been able to use it elsewhere.

By staying close to home, I feel that I have been able to gain a certain confidence which comes from learning challenging new skills in a non-threatening setting. In having both the immediate mental and physical support of my parents, I have learned about my own needs for independence.

Now I look forward to moving away from home, I hope far away, to continue my studies. My search for graduate school has been largely my own. My parents, who spent hours perusing college brochures during my senior year of high school, know nothing about the relative merit of one graduate-level literature program over another. I feel both the anxiety and the excitement of making these decisions alone, of assuming the weight of my own life as I find myself no longer balanced on my parents' shoulders but standing beside them. After graduate school, I may or may not come back to Idaho, but I know that I leave with the confidence of knowledge I have gained here. And if I come back, it will be with the knowledge that I could only gain elsewhere.

Someday Junelle Harris hopes to work for the Peace Corps in a faraway country.

Two

What

Type

Are

You?

3 *the small*
liberal-arts college

The liberal arts were defined by Aristotle and Plato as those subjects which developed intellectual and moral excellence. These subjects included literature, logic, law, music, astronomy, arithmetic, and geometry. Today, liberal-arts colleges continue this tradition, exposing students to courses ranging from Introduction to Geology (a.k.a. Rocks for Jocks) to a seminar on rock-'n'-roll as social protest. All this is offered within a small-campus environment, enabling students to have more access to their professors and more freedom to discuss ideas in class.

In the next essay, Kay Walraven tells what life is like at a small liberal-arts college.

Intensive Care

by Kay Walraven

a viral rash. That was my diagnosis at the Davidson College infirmary, and news of my condition spread faster than the outbreak of red whelps aspiring to cover my body. On voice mail: "Heard you had a rash." On E-mail: "Hope that rash goes away." In the hallway: "How's that rash?" Even a week later, in the library, at the lunch table, at frat parties: "So-and-so said you had a rash. Glad you got rid of it." I fully anticipated radio coverage and a quarter-page bulletin in the school paper so each of the 1,600 students could care. I appreciated the concern, but the attention made me feel even more embarrassed and conspicuous than the rash itself. I could wear all the long-sleeved shirts and jeans I wanted, but there was no hiding.

You don't need a rash to figure out small liberal-arts schools are like that. Don't worry about airing your dirty laundry, it will probably get run up a pole for you. This is not to say your innermost personal life gets broadcast in flashing lights outside the student union, but if you have roommate problems, a car wreck, or get knee-walking drunk, people are going to know. Small schools offer no refuge. Sworn enemies and ex-sweethearts do not wither away. They crop up in classes, at parties, and seemingly around every corner. If you upset a professor or slack off in his or her class, not only will other faculty know, but you are bound to encounter that professor on campus and in the community. Unlike a large school, where you can voice an opinion and then fall back into the comfort of the masses, at a small school, when you stick your neck out, it stays on the chopping block. Locking your door at night after that controversial editorial may not be such a bad idea. People know where you live. People know who you are. Your actions and activities follow you wherever you go. You might be known for taking charge of a community service project, winning second place in the school writing contest, or including purple-polka-dot pants in your wardrobe. Anonymity does not exist, and for some, campus can become a tad claustrophobic.

Small schools are not, however, populated with paranoid pupils. Despite the drawbacks, it's true what they say: good things come in small packages. No matter where you go, you are met with smiles and salutations, and whether you opt for a frat party or turn out for a school-sponsored concert, you can count on being among familiars. The tightness of the social community also spills over into the classroom. Whereas at a large school you may find yourself sitting in a classroom of hundreds, knowing little or nothing about your classmates, at a small school you will sit in a class of ten to thirty and know most people's name, year, major, home state, and extracurriculars. Size and familiarity with other students cultivate a community within the classroom where all students can contribute opinions and perspectives comfortably.

Most of my courses have revolved around discussion. Students and professors circle up and toss ideas into the ring. Questions and comments are not only appreciated but recommended if you expect a healthy class-participation grade at the end of the course. To benefit fully from a dose of discussion, students must open wide and communicate, but also be willing to swallow a few bitter pills along the way. I've gotten myself into a number of scholarly scuffles. The forum format is conducive to debate. But respect and order always prevail. Civil disagreement is part of the process, and besides, professors are always there to referee. Of course, professors do not just sit around officiating student free-for-alls. They lecture and assign papers and tests as any professor would, but at small school, professors do more than teach. They become your friends.

Seeing your professors do the macarena at a party would not be completely out of the ordinary. You would come closer to encountering them at a student/faculty dinner or poetry reading. Friends of mine have gone to concerts and gone shopping with professors. I myself have enjoyed many evenings at professors' homes, small get-togethers and meals. Professors are not guaranteed to be your best pals; some may just as soon throw themselves in front of a car than walk past you on the sidewalk. But, as a rule, professors welcome contact with students, and students treasure the personal attention. The informal relationship that develops between students and professors allows for a more comfortable atmosphere in which students do not feel inferior to or overpowered by faculty. Students feel significant and appreciated. Students feel noticed, and they are.

But when the phone drags you out of bed at 9:35 in the morning, and the voice on the other end may be your professor, who, after noticing your absence in the 8:30 World Music class, decided to check up on your whereabouts with a personalized wake-up call, you think about the large school you opted out of. You don't go to class late. You don't skip class. You don't brush off assignments or do mediocre work. For one, there's that whole failing thing. But the personal attention you receive from professors compels you to do your best, and that includes showing up on time. Close contact with professors is demanding, but well worth the added pressure. Getting called in for a meeting because of less-than-peak performance or concerns about your personal health and well-being is not unusual. I have talked to professors about everything from insecurity to family problems. Professors are usually approachable and eager to talk. Most important, professors let me know I am a person first and a student second, and that has been invaluable throughout my college career.

My biggest concern when applying to college was the "liberal arts" end of the deal. When thinking about small liberal-arts colleges, people often envision droves of private- and boarding-school graduates buzzing around campus in their Beamers and Volvos, chatting on the cell phone with Mommy and Daddy before an afternoon of tennis. If that were the case, my Calhoun, Georgia, Tempo-diving, middle-class self would have gone the university way. Granted small liberal-arts schools tend to be expensive and more selective, and no, you won't find an old clunker in every parking space, but you don't have to be a posh frosh to pass through the front gates. Whether you require financial aid or not, whether you graduate private or public, whether you hail from Pakistan, Park Avenue, or Podunk, you should not rule out a small liberal-arts college on the basis of common, often false, perceptions.

But, to answer the million-dollar question or, more accurately, the approximately $60,000 question: What is a liberal-arts education? I certainly didn't know when I was applying to college, though I thought I did. "Liberal arts" conjured pretentious notions of some supreme intellectual pursuit that would lift me to new heights of wisdom and self-discovery within the cosmos. Socrates and Leonardo da Vinci would welcome me onto campus at freshman orientation, and Aristotle would even carry my bags up the stairs to my dorm room as I started off on the road to becoming a Renaissance woman.

In truth, I wasn't completely off. The liberal-arts curriculum embraces a range of disciplines to equip students with critical ways of thinking, rather than preparing students for one specific profession or field. Logic and reason, not law or engineering. Pre-med and pre-law programs are sometimes offered, but the curriculum tends to be more general. The requirements include math and science, as at most any school, but philosophy, religion, psychology, and fine arts also appear on the list. Buddhist Traditions to Jesus and His Interpreters, Existentialism to Social Deviants, Wild and Edible Plants to Death and Dying. A multitude of courses are open to all students, regardless of major. As an English major, I have taken Modern American Drama, Shakespeare's Contemporaries, and Violence in Drama and Film. I have also been exposed to Speech, Directing, and Petroleum to Penicillin. And I was eventually introduced to Leonardo—in Art 210: Italian Renaissance Painting.

When I flash my liberal-arts credentials in the "real world," it will indicate that I am a well-rounded individual. My liberal-arts education has enabled me to bridge fields of study with a common approach to discovery and learning, and I can apply this skill to everyday life, no matter the situation. My view is not narrow or limited. A method-based, universal curriculum has given me universal access. I may not be an expert on everything, but I can probably scratch the surface.

I would be making a rash recommendation if I prescribed a small liberal-arts education for everyone, or if I suggested the liberal-arts plan as the best education. Large schools offer many things small ones do not—characteristics which, to some, would be appealing. But if you are itching for contagious camaraderie, intensive care, and an expansive examination of courses to cure your every curiosity, a small liberal-arts education may be just what the doctor ordered.

Kay Walraven is an English major at Davidson College.

4 the large
state university

Picture the last concert you went to. Okay, now take out
the mosh pit. Good. Stop the music, turn up the lights,
and ask everyone around you to sit down. Have the band
leave and replace them with a person around forty-five
years old with glasses and a lot of papers. All right, you
may or may not have worn that outfit if you knew you'd
wind up in class—but take out your notebook: you're in the
middle of a lecture at a state university.

Okay, the comparison is not perfect—but it's close. At
a concert, even though you may be front-row center, the
band probably doesn't know who you are. At a state university lecture, even though you're front-row center, the
professor probably doesn't know who you are. And just like
that concert, the class may have hundreds of spaces available, but they go quickly.

Each year, close to 6 million people attend one of the
nation's 605 state universities, where the average com-
bined cost of tuition and room and board is under $7,000
a year. One of those 6 million is Laura Kosa, who, in the
next essay, shows you a different way to live large.

Learning Large

by Laura Kosa

*h*ere I am, at the University of Kentucky, surrounded by four hundred students, all waiting to hear a lecture on corporate finance. We must all be nuts. We're sitting elbow-to-elbow because the seats are so crammed together. Our knees are pulled up to our chests because the rows are so close, to accommodate so many people. The guy that I want to know is sitting seven rows back in the left-hand section. How am I ever going to meet him? And when and if I ever do, how will he remember me from the other 40 million women on this campus? Maybe, like me, he came to UK to get out of Ohio. Maybe he, too, is feeling like a buoy bobbing aimlessly in the sea.

Eleven in the morning—time for class number 2. It's not so bad in here, only forty seats, evenly spaced and more conducive to study. The teacher is old! His views of our generation are as ancient as he looks. According to him, we're all slackers who can't communicate or write. I can tell he'll be a challenge. But I guess the time has come to face up to those challenges if I'm going to make my mark in a pool of twenty-four thousand.

Some days, walking home from class is wonderful, and some days it isn't. If I've had a rough day and I want to be alone during my twenty-minute walk back to South campus, it's not hard to avoid people, because I rarely see anyone I know. I may pass forty or fifty people I've never seen before in my life. But on other days, something exciting may have happened and I want desperately to share it with a friend during the walk home. The days I spot someone are great, but they are few and far between. Usually, I walk briskly back to the residence hall and bolt upstairs to scribble something on my best friend's dry-erase board.

Sure, friends can be found everywhere on this campus. The tricky thing is meeting them. You may have classes with forty to four hundred students. But how do you set aside your fears and walk up to the girls on the intramural field to ask if you can play softball with them? It's hard to do. Many girls avoid this dilemma by pledging a sorority. The sororities join the fraternities for mixers and intramural games, and they offer a steady group to meet with at the library. The girls who participate in the sororities seem to have a smaller image of the university. And if you think about it, it makes a lot of sense. Sororities function like a family, a small, intricate group of people who have similar interests and enjoy one another's company. This aspect of college is really wonderful for those who partake of it. On the other hand, I'm not that intrigued by the Greek system, which is fine; being an independent gives me a better opportunity to take on whatever encounters seem to find me.

Maybe I should go see my accounting professor before I head back to the hall. Maybe I shouldn't. The same thought goes through my head every time I want to go speak to him. I often wonder if he even remembers who I am. He has over fifty people in his class; what would make me stick out in his mind? Then again, if he does remember me and I go see him, he may think twice before giving me my final grade at the end of the semester. Wishful thinking never hurt anyone, and an extra ten minutes added to my walk isn't such a burden.

Mail. I know it comes only once a day, but I find myself looking in my mailbox over and over again, hoping to see *something*. Even a bill would do. Sometimes I think I get more use out of my E-mail address than out of my postal address, and considering how many computer labs and libraries there are on this campus, I can't say I'm ever without a terminal to check my E-mail either. Actually, I've come to love my E-mail address. It keeps me in touch with friends in the North. When I really start to miss people in Ohio or Wisconsin, I'm only a keystroke away. That can be comforting at times, when you need immediate contact with an old friend and the postal service seems just too slow.

Living in the residence halls is interesting. I've never been around so many types of young women in my life. A lot of the girls on my floor are in sororities. They have their doors decorated with their chapter's mascots. Some of the girls are from the same hometowns, which seems to make it easy for them to get a home-away-from-home feeling when they start to miss Mom and Dad. Me, I just roam from group to group, making friends with those who take the time to share a smile. To me, the idea of making totally new friends is exciting and worthwhile. But washing your undergarments in the same machine as 170 other women is a humbling experience. Of course the water is clean, but I still feel uncomfortable removing someone else's panties from the spin cycle that was completed thirty minutes ago and still hasn't been tended to by the rightful user. I mean, my panties need to be washed, too!

Okay, classes are over for the day. My laundry's clean. My mail is checked. What am I forgetting? My stomach. People always worry about the "freshman fifteen," but I don't understand why. I guess it depends on the person, but considering how much brain power I use in my studies, and how many thoughts spin through my head about life in general, I forget to eat sometimes. Luckily, my stomach never hesitates to remind me. Often, the common solution is a bar of chocolate, but the healthy stuff is necessary, too.

I'll rush over to the commons. This is where all the South campus residents eat. Though I would kill for a piece of Mom's lasagna right about now, I have to settle for the same old cafeteria offerings. The Grill line is huge. The weight watchers are huddled around the salad bar. Oh, look! The cute boy from finance is over by Mom's Kitchen. I think I might want pasta, but then again, I had that yesterday. The line at the Asian Corner doesn't look that bad. A fortune cookie might bring me lots of luck; maybe it'll say my social life is about to peak. OK, now that I've got my dinner, I've got to find the friends I came with. We have a deal to save a seat for the poor soul who gets caught in the longest line.

The day is just about over. Actually, it's a beautiful evening for a walk. We could go to the Office Tower or go by the fountain. We could truck all the way over to North campus and visit friends. Sorority circle is also a nice place to walk; the old Tudor homes have a nostalgic old-Kentucky atmosphere. Anywhere we decide to go, it'll be a good long walk. Then it'll be time for homework and finally time for bed! Oh geez, I always forget the most important things I'm supposed to do—and then I remember them when I'm winding down for bed. Spring registration! I can't believe I almost forgot. My window for phone registration opens on Tuesday and I have yet to plot out my schedule. Students usually have a whole list of options readily available in case the dreaded computer voice says, "Sorry, that section is closed." This happens because upperclassmen have top priority and get to register first.

My bed is probably my most prized possession. I use every minute of the day to its full capacity. Either I've walked five miles in one afternoon or I've spent three hours in the library trying to locate one book. Or perhaps I've agonized over my accounting homework for hours and my eyes hurt and I keep cursing my calculator. The cycle never ends, but through it all, my bed is always there at midnight. Warm. Plush. Welcoming. It's a place where I can collect my thoughts. Some nights I'm thankful for the many people and experiences I have encountered. Other nights I contemplate grabbing a plane ticket and flying home for the weekend; these are the nights when I question my happiness here. Some people seem so incredibly happy. Those who are in sororities or who are native Kentuckians and have always dreamed of going to UK seem to embrace every aspect of the university and relish their experiences. I find myself for some reason contemplating transferring and wonder if I could be as happy as they are in another atmosphere. Who knows. It seems that loneliness and excitement go hand in hand.

Right about now, other girls on my floor are congregating at their sorority houses, and others are together, glancing back at their high school yearbooks. I'm just relaxing in my bed, watching Letterman. Only a few hours of pure, peaceful bliss before I'm back in the sea of thousands, staring at a professor who seems to be speaking another language, brushing my elbows with the stranger next to me, and wondering, How am I going to meet that cute guy seven rows back on the left?

Laura Kosa transferred and is now finishing her degree in mass media at the University of Akron, in Akron, Ohio.

the women's college

Before you read the next essay, I want to share with you some findings about coed colleges which may surprise you. Researchers at the American University in Washington, D.C., have found that, in coed classes, men spoke up eight times more often than women. At the Harvard Graduate School of Education, analyizing videotapes of classes at the formerly all-women's Wheaton College after it became coeducational, researchers found that the tiny number of male students dominated classroom discussion and were taken more seriously than the female students only two years after Wheaton began admitting men. University of Illinois researchers found that women's self-esteem tends to drop after they've spent a year in a coed college.

On the other hand, findings about women's colleges are very different. A study of college environments reports, "Single-sex colleges show a pattern of effects . . . that is uniformly positive. Students become academically involved, interact with faculty frequently, show large increases in intellectual self-esteem, and are more satisfied with practically all aspects of the college experience compared with their counterparts in coeducational institutions. Women's colleges increase the chances that women will obtain positions of leadership, complete the baccalaureate degree, and aspire to higher degrees." And a study done by Brown University found that higher than average proportions of women's-college graduates felt that they had gained confidence, were well prepared for graduate studies, and planned to go on to doctoral programs.

Leigh Goldberg didn't have any of this information when she visited a women's college. But she eventually found out why so many women's-college students feel their school would be better dead than coed.

Better Dead Than Coed

by Leigh Goldberg

When I first began the process of looking into colleges, I wasn't considering the women's-colleges route. As a matter of fact, I was insulted when my college counselor listed three women's colleges as possible choices. He said that I would really enjoy a single-sex experience. I didn't think I would. In my mind, women's colleges were too isolated and small. They were where pretentious girls went— the next logical stage in their debutante lives. To me, a women's college meant pink dorm rooms with frilly curtains, house mothers, Miss Manners books on lunchroom tables, and little, if any, social life.

I wanted a school which allowed me to be an individual, not a member of a group. In high school, I was a writer for the school literary magazine, a varsity soccer player, and active in the local music scene. And while I despised the meat-market feel of fraternities, I did want to have lots of male friends, just as I did in high school. Taking these things into account, I thought women's colleges would limit my interests and threaten my social life. I did take my counselor's advice, though, and visited one: Smith.

I stayed with a woman I knew from high school, Alana. I had always admired her but was a little intimidated by her levelheadedness and assertiveness. She was always so successful at everything she did—school, friends, activities. Upon my arrival at Smith, I began to notice that the qualities I admired in Alana were not uncommon in most of the women there. And as the weekend went on, I also realized I was having a lot of fun with Alana and her friends. We ate dinner in the house; the women eat in their own "houses" (note: never call them dorms), and during dinner the women played music on the house jukebox while we talked about current events, academic matters, and weekend plans. Then on Friday afternoon the house had tea together. It is the responsibility of the first-years to serve cookies, vegetables, and beverages to the rest of the women every Friday. This tradition began with the first fourteen women who attended the school. Tea was adapted to include Oprah and MTV, and is meant to provide a transition between the school week and the weekend.

It wasn't until I returned home and answered my family's questions that it hit me—there were no tyrannical house mothers or pink dorm rooms; students studied tons but also had a lot of freedom with their responsibilities; there was not just one type of woman there, and not once had I noticed the absence of men on campus. The visit to Smith was nothing like the culture shock I expected. I decided that Smith was where I belonged.

Many people at my high school reacted to my decision with dyke or feminazi jokes. But I had seen what Smith was, and they hadn't. I knew that I was adding my name to the names of hundreds of important women who had been there, becoming a part of a long legacy. I am now in my third year and know there are things about a women's-college environment you cannot fully appreciate during a weekend visit.

One thing is the classroom experience. Classes at a women's college are quite different from those I attended in my coed high school and in coed colleges. At a women's college, the classroom atmosphere is more relaxed and conducive to asking questions. The classes are very small (my smallest has been four students), and it is hard to avoid being singled out every once in a while. Men who take classes at Smith, which happens quite frequently, must be commended for their bravery. The first time a man speaks in class, it's difficult not to turn around to locate the deepest voice in the room. And we demand that they prove their intellectual abilities along with the rest of us. Sometimes this is difficult; I have noticed that guys act differently in a predominately female setting. Many are very quiet and do not contribute to class discussions. Some sit slouched and act uncomfortable and immature. There are men who come to learn about the particular subject matter, but there are also those who take classes at Smith in order to learn about the inner social workings of the school. But often enough these guys and the people you meet when taking classes through the college consortiums become friends. When I have taken classes at other colleges, I've noticed that female students in these settings don't speak up in class as women do at Smith. When they do, they seem timid and a bit embarrassed. It's odd to see that happen; it's like looking at the way I was in high school. After experiencing the comfort of speaking in all-women classes, I feel just as comfortable speaking in coed settings. I can't imagine feeling embarrassed or censoring myself because men are around.

Speaking about men being around, we have formal winter and spring weekends, during which men come from all over the Northeast with brothers, cousins, and high school buddies to be entertained by the hostesses for the weekend. Many are disappointed by the number of men in attendance; to some guests, the competition is an unwelcome surprise. The festivities at Smith are different from those at coed schools; each house has any combination of cocktail, dance, and after-hour parties on formal weekends. Every student that chooses to become a social member has a job at every party; they answer the door, check guest lists, and escort non-house members to bathrooms and through hallways. The house works together to ensure that every party is as safe as it is fun. Men often stay in the rooms of the women who invite them for the weekend (there is only one rule about overnight guests—they cannot stay for more than twenty-eight days in one semester). But there are guest rooms in each house where men may also stay. Many men opt for these: sometimes sharing a bathroom with forty-plus women is a bit overwhelming for them. The men in attendance are charmed by our maturity, manners, intelligence, and ability to put a roomful of guys at ease. You have to be invited to our parties, and many of the guys comment that it is a valuable connection to have and ask to be included in future events. I have been to parties at coed colleges and have seen how men behave in those settings. Maybe they are reacting to the fact that we have consciously chosen a college which excludes them, but at our formals it does seem as if the maturity level rises and men treat us by a set of higher standards than they do our coed counterparts.

And when the men are gone Smith becomes a women's college again. The friendships that exist among women, when men are absent from the equation, are completely different from relationships created in the coed world. It's as if women do not listen to each other when men are around. That won't happen here. The idea of sisterhood is a foreign one to many; I am positive I would not fully understand it had I not attended a women's college. Here there are so many divisions in the group formerly known as simply "women"; we are athletes, scholars, feminists, anti-feminists, pro-life, pro-choice, Democrats, Republicans, artists, writers, scientists. And all of us eat together, joke together, and sometimes even go to class in our pajamas, together. But we also have disagreements—and the campus has been the setting of several controversies.

Each year on Coming-Out Day, for example, the lesbian population "chalks" the campus sidewalks and brick buildings with statements about their freedom and gay pride. While some heterosexual students decorate the campus with supportive banners for their "out" friends, many heterosexuals who aren't necessarily homophobic protest the sometimes offensive artwork. My first year of college, Coming-Out Day coincided with Parents' Weekend. Of course, our house had been decorated with colored chalk, and a strategically placed inscription of one woman's pride in being a "vagitarian" graced our front steps. My parents, hoping to understand collegiate lingo, were curious about the term. I have to say that my parents handled my answer very well; my father coughed and Mom politely averted her eyes from the sidewalk.

That same year, however, the majority of our campus joined forces against a professor who published work espousing the idea that intelligent women, such as those at Smith, should be "breeders," staying at home and giving birth to intelligent children. Some women at school were more aggressive than others in their protest. After having his office broken into and hate mail sent to his home, the professor issued a statement saying that he did not feel "safe" at Smith. So, sometimes we do fight each other; other times we bond together against an "evil force" or lend our energies to larger issues.

At a women's college, what matters most is how you think, what you do, and who you are, not what you look like or who you know. Our professors respect us, not as women, but as scholars. Affirmative action is a major issue on the outside, but at a women's college you will never get a job, praise, or attention for being a woman—because we are all women. You will be singled out only if you are worthy.

One criticism leveled against women's colleges is that women don't learn to compete with men. My response is this: when I leave Smith, I leave with a knowledge of self-worth. I expect to be seen by others as who I am inside— and not as simply a gender. I will not see those I work with, compete with, and have fun with as simply men or women. I will see them as scholars, writers, artists, Democrats, feminists . . . all the categories I have learned that people fall into. And by evaluating people as who they are and according to what they do, I will always be blessed with meaningful relationships and the rewarding feeling of knowing exactly who I am. I will have learned all of this from a women's college.

Leigh Goldberg is an English major with a minor in Jewish studies.

6

lesbianism and the women's college

Mention going to a women's college and there is a chance someone will make a comment about lesbianism. Why? Are there a lot of lesbians at women's colleges? Actually, there is no evidence that there are more at either women's colleges or coed ones. As a matter of fact, 75 percent of women's-college graduates marry and about half have children. Also, statistically, their marriages last longer than those of their coed counterparts. So why does this idea persist? Perhaps it's that lesbians at women's colleges are the only people who can have intimate relationships with their classmates. So maybe it's just that lesbianism is more obvious when men are subtracted from the equation.

Lily Chiu came to a women's college feeling very secure about her heterosexuality. Then one day her roommate confessed her homosexual feelings, and everything changed.

My Roommate Thinks She's a Lesbian

by Lily Chiu

*a*s a senior in high school, I had a hard time deciding between two colleges. One was an Ivy League and the other was a women's college. The Ivy League boasted a big name and prestige. The drawback, however, was the size. I couldn't get used to the idea that some of the lecture classes might have up to four hundred students. The women's college was more to my liking: only 2,700 undergraduates, and a low student-to-faculty ratio. On the other hand, the women's college wasn't as prestigious as the Ivy League, despite the fact it was a Seven Sisters school.

Even after hours of making meticulous lists of the pros and cons for both schools, I still couldn't make up my mind. So I started asking advice from my teachers and friends. Today, three years later, one piece of advice sticks out in my mind. It was from one of the guys in my AP French class—the guy I then had a huge crush on, in fact. I told him my dilemma; he listened courteously, then uttered his opinion: "Don't go to a women's college. You'll come out a lesbian!"

It amused me when I heard him say that. From his point of view, women's colleges were factories where women went in as heterosexuals and emerged as lesbians. But then I started wondering. Lesbianism was simply not one of the things I'd thought about in high school. Sure, there were rumors about girls in my class, but I'd had doubts about their legitimacy. The high school I went to was pretty shielded from this nasty thing called lesbianism. So when this guy I was attracted to actually brought up the L-word, I was forced to confront it. I hadn't realized the full implications of attending a women's college. I accessed my memory banks, searching for the details of my visit to the campus. Had I seen any lesbians while I was there? Had I talked to any? If I had, why didn't I realize it?

Despite all these daunting considerations, I decided to go to the women's college after all, and was promptly placed in a lesbian house—that is, a dorm in which a lot of lesbians lived. The first person I met when moving in was one of my HONS (Heads of New Students), who had pink hair, a nose ring, and a freedom-rings necklace (though I had no idea what it was at the time). After my initial wariness, I began to grow accustomed to the sight of nose rings, freedom rings, pink triangles, women with short hair, women who kissed each other, butch lesbians, and femme lesbians. I learned what a lambda sign meant and what labrys was. I started substituting "significant other" for boyfriend or lover. You name it, I wasn't fazed by it. Even the fact that our head resident and our house president were lovers wasn't so terribly disturbing to me—after the first month or so. I was proud of having adjusted to a lesbian atmosphere so quickly.

In my newfound lesbian awareness, I thought nothing could shock me. I was wrong. One morning, my roommate Diane told me she thought she was a lesbian. I listened to her explain her crush on Karen, one of the women in our house, and I was amazed to find myself envious of her. I, too, had a crush on one of our housemates, but I had explained this sapphic attraction to myself in a very logical, methodical, almost scientific way. Observation: I was attending a college with no guys. Observation: I still needed "crushes" to make life interesting and bearable. Hypothesis: I developed a crush on a woman. And to support my brilliant hypothesis was the undeniable fact that the object of my diffident interest looked like a beautiful boy. (In fact, now that I think about it, she looked quite a bit like my AP French crushee. I wonder what he'd have thought of that.)

I flatter myself that I took Diane's announcement pretty much in stride. The woman she had a crush on looked very much like a guy, too. Later on, I found out that almost half of the other first-years had a crush on her as well. I considered explaining my theory of why we were attracted to these lesbians (for surely they were lesbians) to my roommate, but I didn't. I didn't want to spoil her newfound revelation (she called it love) with prosaic logic.

For the rest of the semester I watched as the puppy love grew. Diane broke off with her boyfriend of three years, a very sweet guy, from what I could tell. She told him the truth—that she was in love with a woman. He took it well, considering. Perhaps he, like my AP French crushee, also knew that everyone who went to a women's college would come out a lesbian. Once that was behind her, Diane started working toward her goal. She bought herself a freedom-rings necklace, as well as several books on homosexuality. She started hanging out with other lesbians in the house. She talked to the object of her desire a lot and reported their conversations back to me. I listened, living vicariously through her experiences. My own loved one had been spending a lot of time with one of the other first-years, who was also a lesbian. There were rumors that they were a couple. I was jealous, but too shy and uncertain to do anything about it. That's why I admired Diane so much when she left Karen a rose with a note explaining her feelings for her.

What Karen said to Diane upon receiving the gift and confession I never knew. I passed them talking together in the foyer, both with serious expressions on their faces. Much as I wanted to stop and eavesdrop, I willed myself to keep walking. Later that night, Diane told me part of their conversation. Her love was unrequited. Karen was flattered and touched but did not return Diane's emotions.

I don't know if Diane stopped regarding herself as a lesbian then. To tell the truth, I didn't notice much. It was finals time, and I was too busy trying catch up on all the work I hadn't done during the semester to worry about Diane's state of mind. So it came as a surprise when, after winter break, she announced that she wasn't a lesbian anymore. She'd gotten back together with her ex-boyfriend over break and apparently had realized that she was still attracted to him. She came back to school understandably confused about her sexuality. She'd firmly believed herself heterosexual for eighteen years, suddenly found herself attracted to women for four months, but then, to her dismay, caught herself loving a man again. Two days after she told me this, I came home from class and found her packing her stuff. She was leaving school, she told me. And three days later, she did.

And now, almost three years later, I'm still trying to figure out what happened then. I also left school at the end of my first year, because of personal problems, and spent the first semester of my sophomore year at home. The casualty rate in my house among the first-years was high. Out of sixteen of us, only four opted to stay in the house. Some of us moved to other houses, some had transferred to other schools, some, like Diane and me, had left indefinitely. I don't think the lesbian issue had anything to do with it; all the first-year lesbians left the house, and the four students who stayed were comfortably heterosexual. I'm sure a lot of it had to do with the lack of good guidance, since our head resident and house president spent most of the time holed up in the head resident's suite together and didn't pay as much attention to us as they probably should have.

But, for me at least, I think the real problem was that I lost myself in the glamour of it all. It sounds strange to hear it put that way, I know, but that's really the closest I can get to describing it. I remember once, in sex-ed class in high school, watching a video of a homosexual describing what it was like to be gay. "Imagine yourself, a heterosexual, being in a world of homosexuals. Everyone around you is gay. You are the only one who is not." This hypothetical scenario came true for me, as well as for Diane and most of the first-years in our house. In this brave new world, being lesbian was cool. And I felt gauche and left out. I didn't want to be labeled what Diane's gay friend disdainfully called "H-squared"—Hopelessly Heterosexual.

I read recently in a magazine that homosexuality and bi-sexuality are very much in fashion now. In vogue or not, I admired (and still do) the lesbians I know for their courage, their radicalness, their defiance. I suppose, in some way, I wanted those qualities to be my own, and that's why I, Diane, and others wanted so much to be lesbians. Some of us, like Diane, went to the point of believing ourselves homosexual. Others, such as the so-called four-year lesbians, resorted to "passing" for homosexual: having lesbian relationships while in college, and then reassuming a hetero-sexual role after graduation. Some played at being lesbians—like my friend and her roomie holding hands just to make a statement. And still others, and I fall into this category, were just plain confused about their sexual inclination.

I can't tell you what happened to Diane, exept that she's back at Smith, living in the same house as I am, and I see her every day. What I can tell you is what happened to me. After my semester away from school, I came back and was placed in another house—a house which wasn't especially noted for the sexual orientation of its residents, one way or the other. There are lesbians in the house, but it wasn't a big deal. I actually got to know these lesbians, instead of worshipping them from afar and having crushes on them. I'm not friends with these women because they are lesbians; I'm friends with them because I like them and feel comfortable around them. And, with them, I don't feel the pressure to categorize myself or others.

I'm glad I go to a women's college, and I am grateful I was placed in a lesbian house my first year. Without that experience, I'd never have gained an insight into what true acceptance is—not only acceptance of others but also, and more important, acceptance of oneself. And if I ever bump into my former AP French crushee and he asks me if I turned out to be a lesbian, I know what I'll do: smile enigmatically at him and simply walk away. Let the boy wonder.

Lily Chiu plans on becoming an English professor and hopes to teach at a women's college.

the ivy league

Harvard, Princeton, Yale, Brown, Columbia, Cornell, Dartmouth, University of Pennsylvania. This is the Ivy League.
And though each has a distinct personality, the association they share, the small pool of people they accept (on
average, 23 percent), and the prestigious reputations they
uphold form a strong base of similarity. In the following
essay, Julia Lee explains how an Ivy League education can
be both rewarding and stifling.

A League of Their Own

by Julia Lee

My Princeton interview was an unqualified disas-
ter: I was sick and sniffling, and the local interviewer was
forced to pause every few minutes for me to blow my nose
and wipe my eyes. In between coughs and sneezes, she managed to ask, "So where does Princeton rank among schools
you've applied to?" I hedged, because I really didn't know.
So when she predicted, "I bet you'll probably stay close to

home; go to a state school," I figured that she had effectively sealed my fate. I didn't think I wanted to leave California for New Jersey, but hell, it was a renowned Ivy League institution, so I might as well apply. When I got my acceptance letter, I decided to visit Princeton to see for myself whether my interviewer was right and I should stick with the safe and familiar.

Immediately upon arriving at the campus, I was struck by how beautiful and steeped in tradition everything was. After all, my high school's pride in its hundred-year existence was dwarfed by Princeton's 250. The novelty of it all impressed me; from the flagstone walkways to the carved initials on old woodwork to the preppy men's a cappella groups.

Suddenly I could also become part of this breathlessly elite school, and even before I arrived back home, I had decided to take the opportunity. And I admit, there was a smug satisfaction in answering "Princeton University" to people's inquiries of where I was matriculating. The hard part seemed to be over—I had survived the rigorous admissions process, and now I simply had to get myself over there in the fall.

Nonetheless, I started my first day of classes with more than my share of trepidation. What if high school was a breeze compared to college? Geniuses were supposed to attend the Ivy Leagues, and I certainly wasn't one. In the end, however, academics was the least hairy of the transitions from high school. I soon learned that there would always be those who were superhumanly brilliant, but the majority of my classmates were of fairly normal, if above average, intelligence.

The common perception is that SAT scores and GPA essentially determine your acceptance, but the diversity of the student body undermines this theory. And this was my greatest surprise in freshman year; like a state school, Princeton has its share of jocks. And while most of these recruited athletes were comparably smarter than their counterparts at scholarship schools, their presence definitely affected the academic environment. The jocks range from those with backwards baseball hats who unembarrassedly admit, "I'm here to play volleyball" (or lacrosse or football), to true scholar-athletes who managed to qualify for NCAA finals while simultaneously writing a high-honors thesis. Sure, the jock presence exists at all schools (the drunken initiation or hazing rites for new team members, the suffering of academics for the rigors of athletic practice, the domination of the social scene), but perhaps the jock presence is more acutely felt at Princeton precisely because it seems almost incongruous among the gothic architecture and carefully tended lawns.

The other significant factor in the Princeton student body is the legacy student. Because it is an Ivy League with an enormous number of alums, Princeton invests much to preserve alumni loyalty. And almost everywhere you look, there is someone whose father or grandfather was a Princeton graduate. Princeton, like other Ivy Leagues, admits to having a policy of legacy preference. In other words, when two equally qualified applicants come up for reviews, one candidate's legacy connection may prove the deciding factor in his or her being accepted over the other. These legacy students may have been raised surrounded by Princeton regalia, attending reunions, and knowing the campus with great familiarity. It is quite common to walk into a person's bedroom and note a huge banner from the Class of '65 hanging on the wall. The current dean of admissions has gradually decreased the number of legacy students, but their numbers remain significant.

Coupled with the small size of the school and the strenuous admissions process, Princeton ensures a rabidly loyal following. Princeton T-shirts, hats, and other paraphernalia decorate almost every student. The summer before I left for school, I was working on a community-service project when the L.A. mayor, Richard Riordan, dropped by for a brief photo op. When I introduced myself as a Princetonian, Riordan immediately began to reminisce fondly about his alma mater. The following summer, as I was applying for a job at a clothing store, a customer overheard me tell the manager that I go to Princeton; immediately she introduced herself as an alum and asked if she could take me out to lunch sometime to chat.

But there does exist a downside to the insularity and tradition of Princeton. Sure, it may be nice to walk past the buildings that figure so prominently in F. Scott Fitzgerald's *This Side of Paradise*. But the elitist institutions and practices so omnipresent in Fitzgerald's Princeton memoirs *also* still exist. Take the eating clubs: as bastions of exclusivity and tradition, they operate as social and eating facilities for the Princeton student body. Some of the clubs still practice a controversial selection process called "bicker," appropriately named to describe the bickering within the club as they select potential members. Sound ridiculous and antiquated to posture and please in order to *eat* somewhere? Well, Fitzgerald commented that "the influential man was the non-committal man, until at club elections sophomore year every one should be sewed up in some bag for the rest of his college career." And so the Princeton eating-club system fragments the community even as school pride unifies it.

Entering my junior year, I am considering the various eating options: eating club, cooperative, independent foraging for food, or the university dining services (six dining halls run by the university). At best, an eating club would give me a place to meet friends, have a drink in the tap room, play a game of pool. At worst, it could be a socially exclusive and stifling environment—a true "club." In addition, since the eating clubs serve as social as well as dining facilities, fees can be extremely high ($4,000 to $5,000 per year). But even with the high annual fees, the vast majority of Princeton students join an eating club—over 90 percent. Since upperclassmen and lowerclassmen are already segregated (freshmen and sophomores live in "colleges" and must eat in the university dining halls), the transition to junior year almost makes an eating club a necessity. As an established and accepted location for upperclassmen to eat, the clubs wield a quasi-monopoly.

Princeton is suffused in tradition. Like most Ivy Leagues, Princeton has a history of being the expected destination of many East Coast prep-school kids. And the legacy of such a past remains robust, as students accustomed to the prestige and elitism of boarding school slip easily into the similar world of Princeton. After all, many of these students are following in the steps of their fathers and grandfathers, and the institutions they join and perpetuate remain strikingly unchanged. Princeton only went coeducation in 1970, lending a distinctively masculine flavor to the school. This is most blatant in the eating clubs, where males dominate. Hazing and fraternity bonding rituals are common in certain clubs, and such an atmosphere lends itself to sexist remarks and even harassment. And while the faculty is becoming diversified, most professors tend to be older white males.

My biggest disappointment is that although Princeton definitely flaunts a "smarter" student body, this does not necessarily mean a more *intellectual* student body. We are not a school consisting solely of scholars, philosophers, scientists, and thinkers seized by a desire to learn. We are mostly a bunch of more-or-less well-rounded kids, with many excellent athletes and many pre-professional students who work hard *and* play hard. Monday through Thursday is comprised of harried preparation for class, finishing off lab reports and papers, completing seminar reading, and frantically studying for exams. But Thursday to Sunday may be spent in an alcoholic haze before the ever-present conscience kicks in on Sunday morning. Princeton does not promote a moderate environment; rather, most students apply their energy with a single-minded intensity to everything they do, including partying.

So is the Ivy League truly overrated? I'd say that the prestige and image factor does a pretty good job of painting an exceptionally rosy picture of the school, but the resources and pure power Princeton wields are undisputed. I've had the opportunity to work with many academic heavyweights: people whose books you have read. Princeton maintains a commitment to undergraduate teaching, and no experience better portrays this than a history class I took my freshman year.

The course was called the History of France 1685–1800, and it was taught by Robert Darnton, a foremost scholar of French cultural history. Of course, I didn't realize this at the time: to me, he seemed an extremely likable and easily approachable teacher. As we chatted with him, one of my friends broached the topic of music, especially music of the period Darnton was teaching. And before either of us knew what was happening, Darnton had enlisted our musical interest to lead our own personal lecture on baroque music for the course. Standing before the lectern onstage, facing my entire history class, I couldn't believe that I, a lame freshman, was giving a lecture. But the real treat came afterwards. In thanks for our guest lecture, Darnton took my friend and me to lunch at the posh Prospect House, Woodrow Wilson's residency when he served as Princeton's president. Over omelettes and crab cakes, he took an active interest in our studies and commented on his own education. (He went to Andover, then Harvard, then Oxford as a Rhodes Scholar before arriving at Princeton. Whew!) Even today, as I glance through the newspaper and see him win yet another book prize or honor, I think of the man who generously extended himself to two eager freshmen.

There are many other famous or notable people. John Nash, who won the 1994 Nobel Prize in Economics, frequently walks around campus. Toni Morrison, another Nobel laureate, teaches a few classes every term. My "college" (dormitory) is named for Malcolm "Steve" Forbes '70, former presidential hopeful, multimillionaire, and editor of *Forbes* magazine. His daughter now lives on my floor; she has accompanied her father on the campaign trail for most of the semester. Perhaps the most famous recent Princeton graduates are Brooke Shields '87, Dean Cain '88, and David Duchovny '81. Yes, we have our share of celebrities. Queen Noor '76 has sent her son, Prince Ali Hussein '99, to her alma mater. It's a kick to check out his picture in the student directory: "H.R.H. (His Royal Highness) Ali Hussein, The Royal Palace, Jordan." His bodyguards accompany him to all classes and park their white Lincoln town car in one of the college courtyards.

Princeton absolutely consumes your existence, essentially ensuring your success in life. The alumni network will always be there to catch you, and the connections you make during your four years offer you blatant advantage over other college graduates. But this nurturing and protection can easily become stifling, and there is less room to forge out independently and rebelliously. I feel myself being nudged toward "safer" careers like law or business, and I've noticed a perceptible shift in the way I act, the way I dress, the way I think. I've become "polished," ready to embark smoothly on a successful career, sheltered by the elegant Princeton campus. But in sheltering and nurturing me, has Princeton limited me? My first year, I took economics to prepare for "the future," rather than pursuing creative writing; I participated in the eating-club scene rather than spurning it: I played it safe. But as I spend more time here, I'm gradually learning to test the waters and assert my independence. I see friends at other schools embracing a bohemian, alternative life-style that does not exist at Princeton. Princeton *is* tradition, both inspiring and stifling, and like all other Ivy Leaguers, one must learn to dispense with the stoginess while retaining the vitality which has marked the school for 250 years.

Julia Lee will graduate with a degree in English in 1998.

the black college

The days when black colleges were needed are over. That's what some people contend. After all, since you can choose from every college in the country, why limit yourself to institutions which were created to fill a need that no longer exists? The truth, though, is that it's hard to argue with the results of black colleges. They have much more success retaining and graduating black students than any other type of college. As a matter of fact, even though there are only 107 historically black colleges and universities in the United States (that equals only 3 percent of the nation's colleges), they graduate more than 30 percent of all black graduates annually. Three out of four of all African-Americans with Ph.D.s did their undergraduate work at black colleges. And the four colleges to send the highest number of black students to medical school were Xavier, Howard, Spelman, and Morehouse—all historically black colleges. These aren't the only things that make black colleges unique; 60 percent of students are the first in their families to attend college. And while there are just as many parties and social choices as at any other college, black colleges had the lowest rate of binge drinking.

   Maybe a black college is one of your choices. If so, Anika Simmons can imagine what it will be like for you.

The Blacker the College, the Sweeter the Knowledge

by Anika Simmons

*a*s you thumb through a brochure for Howard University, you weigh the consequences of going there. Your parents/uncle/teacher/cousin/sister attended it and, in a way, you feel obligated to follow in their footsteps. But that isn't the only reason you consider going there. You think about Howard's reputation as one of the best historically black universities around. You've read about its founding and development and you would like to be part of that tradition. You remember, with a slight smirk on your face, that all your friends wear Howard sweatshirts and that the Allen sisters (Debbie and Phylicia) graduated from there, along with a host of other famous people. Your friends would be so jealous if you went there. And the rumors of social life at Howard, having trickled down to you from several reliable sources, make you think that you would have a ball there—in addition to a great education, of course.

You decide that Howard will be the first step in your journey to your dreams. After a frantic final high school semester, a long-awaited graduation, and an anxious summer, you arrive in Washington, D.C., to begin your college career. You walk through the halls of your dormitory, probably the historic Harriet Tubman Quadrangle, a collection of five buildings arranged in a square (it allows no overnight coed visitation, by the way). You meet your roommate and squirm under the critical gaze of her parents.

The first thing that strikes you as you set out to explore the campus is the plethora of black faces. You knew you were coming to a black college, but now what that means dawns on you. You wonder how it will be not to have anyone white in your classes. Mixed feelings of anxiety and delight grab you. On one hand, that is a good thing: you will not be the sole black person in your classes anymore; no one will expect you to represent the entire race; you won't feel the twang of shame and pain when you discuss slavery in history class—and then feel guilty for what you didn't say. On the other hand, that may not be as good as it sounds. You'll have to stand as an individual if everyone is black. Before, it was easy to make friends, to decide which group to hang out with—you automatically bonded with the other blacks in high school. But now? Your friends at predominately white colleges returned home with stories of all-black gatherings in the cafeteria, at the bus stop, in dormitories. At Howard, that won't be the case. You worry about finding a niche and making friends here.

But you have college business to handle. Registration. Meeting people. Course selection. Speaking of courses, once you look through the course booklet and speak with your adviser, you have another revelation. The courses here are so unusual, so different. You keep these thoughts to yourself because you don't want to seem too ignorant about black history. You sign up for Black Diaspora, even though you're not too sure what diaspora means exactly. Specialized classes such as Black Social and Political Protest or Blacks in Antiquity or Contemporary Slavery surprise you; you didn't realize that people studied these things. When you actually start classes, you realize that the curriculum is centered on you, your people and their experiences. *Revelations*, your book from English class, features an excerpt from Malcolm X's autobiography. Your classes instill a sense of pride and an energy in you that you never experienced before. You might experience some anger here, since you understandably feel duped by your high school teachers. They never encouraged you to learn about people like Ida B. Wells, Kwame Nkrumah, or even Toni Morrison, for that matter.

Another strange thing about your new environment is the upperclassmen. After all, you've never seen black people who carry bottles of distilled water around or who come to class with their heads covered every day. Where you come from, all girls have relaxers—none of them wear their hair as short as boys do or in dreadlocks. You meet positive people from Africa, the Caribbean, and the inner cities of the United States. As you meet more and more people who show depth and diversity, you have no choice but to reevaluate some of your preconceived ideas of what it means to be black. You find out that everyone did not come from a Christian home as you did. Some people belong to the Nation of Islam. Others do not even believe in God. While you were raised to eat meat with every meal, some of your friends have been vegetarians since birth.

These people not only cause you to adjust your ideas of black people; they lead you to reconsider your own position in the world. You ask yourself where you belong in this new world you've discovered. Your style, your philosophy, your religion, even your sexuality—everything will be questioned. The only thing you can be sure about is that college will change you.

And it does. Slowly your new environment starts to feel like a better fit. You walk across the yard with confidence now, feeling a part of the university community. By the time your sophomore and junior years roll around, you are a seasoned veteran on campus. You've joined and quit a few clubs and served as an officer in at least one of them. Your core group of friends has probably changed since freshman year, but you are still enjoying yourself. It is also around this time that you realize that the school is not an idyllic haven. Some of the staff in the registrar's or bursar's offices are always rude. It is rare to find a student that has not been the victim of an oversight by the financial-aid office. And sometimes, just sometimes—like when dorms continue to rot and your tuition continues to rise—you and your fellow students wonder exactly what the university spends its money on.

On the brighter side, you discover that many of your professors are extremely helpful. They seem genuinely to care what happens to you. In very few classes are you just a name or number. In fact, you soon learn that being in class can be a bonding experience. In most classrooms, especially where the professors encourage interesting debates, there is a strong sense of community among the students. You notice that even in the larger lecture classes you click with your classmates so well that when you see them outside class you feel comfortable enough to strike up a conversation.

As a seasoned upperclassman, you naturally do what other upperclassmen do—you start to categorize people on campus. The power-mongers are the students most likely to run for a leadership position on campus (student body president, undergraduate trustee). These are the future politicians and lawyers, and for some reason they are all in Greek organizations. You can spot the artsy people just as easily. They hang out on the steps of the fine-arts building, attend plays and poetry readings, smoke cigarettes, and wear retro clothes. Likewise, you know how to distinguish the Christians, the revolutionaries, the athletes, the athletes' groupies, and all the other subgroups.

Last but not least are the party animals. This includes, but is not limited to, the hip-hop fanatics. You learn soon enough that you can count on them to know where the parties are. And since the school is in a large city, these parties are usually not on campus. Only freshmen go to campus-sponsored parties. You chuckle, remembering the days when you danced all night in the student center. But you don't necessarily have to go to any clubs to participate in the social life here; football and basketball games are just as satisfying. You find out through experience that your real matriculation occurs only after you learn the songs and the school's signature dances.

But even with all the categories you set up, you know there is an unspoken code that most of the students, if not all of them, share. This common belief, which bonds you to your peers, is that you should always be aware of the oppression and triumphs, past and present, of African-Americans in this country. In practical terms, this means you resent the LAPD, especially Mark Fuhrman. You don't include Clarence Thomas on your list of heroes. It means you take pride in the accomplishments of African-Americans and you respect Martin Luther King, Jr., and Malcolm X. It means you know something about African history, at least a little more than you knew in high school. It means you acknowledge that racism exists, but you don't use it as an excuse not to try.

These "rules" are not as restrictive as they might sound; most students find it easy to adhere to them and still preserve their individuality. (Those who don't usually don't hang around too long.) You find there is still space to appreciate music, art, or movies not created by blacks. You can have white friends without being treated as if you have the plague. There is even room for you to express your opinions about O. J.'s guilt, if you feel that way.

The more basketball games you attend and clubs you join, the more you care about the university. In many ways, it grows closer to your heart and becomes part of your identity. You become protective and defensive of the school, financial-aid mishaps and crappy dorms aside. You become sensitive to the problems and controversies surrounding the university. The pressure for the university to integrate causes you some stress. It worries you that there is a push for university officials to admit more non-black students; you feel that it might cause your school to lose some of its specialness. And you love defending Howard against attacks that it promotes segregation. You know the school does not discourage whites from attending; it just wants to remain a nurturing environment for black students.

But at the same time personal issues arise while you are here. Sometimes these hit home more than the issues facing the entire school. Like, how do you reconcile being black with being female? Which is more important? Does one even have to be more important? You may also find it hard to fit the values you were raised with into your new perspective on life. Now you might think of sex as a form of expression that is not necessarily shared only with the person you will marry. Maybe you don't want to get married anymore, or at least not upon graduation as you thought you did when you entered the university. Perhaps now the idea of being on your own for a while or traveling around the world is not so scary.

And as your college experience comes to an end, you look back to see specifically what being at a black college did for you. A black college education didn't teach you that you could succeed only in a community of blacks. But it did give you a time to build, to learn, and to prepare for something bigger. Most important, it gave you a chance to be judged by merit. The existence of the "real world" outside these walls was never denied. In fact, the black college always dangled that "real world" in front of you as a goal, a target. But for four years you had a chance to view the "real world" from a haven. For four years, you had a home.

Anika Simmons recently graduated from Howard University and is now completing a master's degree in education.

9

the
community college

Community colleges are for kids who come to school stoned, skip classes, and spend most of the day hanging out under the bleachers. No way would you go to a community college, especially since you can get into a "real" college.

But there are a few things you should know. The first is that community colleges are not for the worst students in high school. As a matter of fact, studies have found that students who transfer from community colleges to four-year colleges achieve consistently higher grades than those who start out at the four-year schools as freshmen. Not only that. Many are fulfilling similar core requirements to those that have to be taken at "real" colleges, but they're doing it for less than $1,500 a year (compared to $6,000 to $15,000 at four-year schools). President Clinton has proposed to make the first year of community college free for all high school graduates from families with an annual income of less than $100,000. The government picks up the tab for your second year as well if you earn a B average or better during your first year. That math says you could save up to $21,000.

But community colleges are different from four-year colleges. Many of the faculty are part-time, there are no *dorms, and a lot of the students are older than twenty-one and coming back to school to learn new skills. Yet, knowing all these differences, Carla Bass, an honor student, chose a community college. In the following essay, she tells you why she'd do it again.*

The Two-Year Itch

by Carla Bass

bracing for the inevitable "Oh, are you still at that community college?" I watched my old high school classmate tug at her UT Austin sweatshirt as she filled me in on the details of her first semester at a big state university.

"I love having my own apartment, and my roommate is really cool," she said, shifting her shopping bag from one hand to the other. "I really didn't even want to come home for Christmas break, but my parents were driving me nuts about it."

Hordes of other college students, looking like sweatshirt ambassadors for every major university in the country, swarmed around us through their old hometown mall.

"Are you still living with your parents? Going to TJC?"

My affirmative answer solicited a sympathetic nod. "Well, maybe you can transfer early, or something. Hey, it was good running into you. I'll try to catch you sometime before I leave again!"

Another hit-and-run, poor-thing-she's-still-at-a-junior-college encounter left me feeling like the kid sister who has to stay home while the big boys go off to play. One of my high school teachers used to joke about Tyler Junior College being "thirteenth and fourteenth grades." I was an honor student, and this comment made me wonder if I was selling myself short by choosing a junior, or "community," college. My friends who went off to school seemed to be heading for new and exciting destinations, pushing away from the safe harbor of parents and home, while I was dog-paddling in the same spot.

"I'm thinking about transferring to a senior university one year early," I mentioned to a friend in the student center on the first day of my second semester. She was one of the so-called non-traditional students, which meant she wasn't eighteen years old, she scheduled her classes around her children's after-school soccer practices, and was much more outspoken in class than the rest of us. The first time I walked into a class that had several students older than my mother, it seemed a little strange. This feeling faded quickly when I realized they provided formidable competition in the classroom and were good study partners. Many of these students, like my friend who already had a degree but had returned to school to make a career change, often gave more down-to-earth advice than my twenty-something friends.

"You want to leave your clean, comfortable home so you can live in a place where you spend your nights fighting for the bathroom instead of studying? Adjusting to living on your own takes up a lot of time, and I think it's easier to concentrate on academics when you're living with family." Along with increasing numbers of displaced homemakers, workers seeking new job skills, and other adult students at community colleges, she understood the stress of managing a household, a job, and a course load. "I agree you need to leave the nest sometime, but staying here one more year would help your parents pay the low-cost tuition."

I was caught between feelings of being left behind by my friends who were at senior universities and the rationale that TJC provided a quality, affordable education while I completed my basic courses. I had heard of and met successful community-college alumni. University personnel had told me that transfers often do better than four-year students during their junior and senior years. Interrupting my decision-making process, my friend asked, "But you think you're missing out on the atmosphere, traditions, and prestige of a nationally known school, don't you?"

She went to pick her children up from school, leaving me with the decision to make and a pile of transfer materials that were getting heavier and more complicated by the minute. One of the biggest hassles at a community college is keeping up with what courses the senior university of choice will accept. I had already gotten lists from my future college of which classes to take if I wanted to earn a degree in four years. By requesting these lists regularly by phone from the dean's office of the senior university I planned on transferring to, I had a steady supply of these ever-changing core-curriculum lists flowing into my mailbox. Since my junior college and senior university don't use the same numbers and abbreviations for equivalent courses, I faced the added task of translating the two systems. Although I would rather render Greek into Chinese, a course-equivalency guide from the senior college's admissions office has been a life saver.

Since my goal at junior college was to take all the general classes—meaning those required outside of my major—I toted my degree plan and course-equivalency guide around to every registration and followed it to the letter. Since many of these courses would apply to several different majors, I tried to stick with the basics and maybe one majors course per semester. My junior college had assigned a counselor to help me, but I also double-checked, calling and talking with an admissions counselor at my senior college.

General degree requirements are the same at many universities, so students can start taking basic courses before they decide where they want to transfer. But knowing your major and the school you want to transfer to helps. I have heard horror stories of uncertain students who repeatedly change majors or their choice of senior college and lose up to twelve hours—a semester's worth of classes. But students who start as freshmen in a senior college run the same risk if they can't make up their minds.

"Hey, guess what?" one of my friends, a prime example of an intelligent but not too certain student, said as he slid into the chair across from me. "I'm changing my major again. Business this time." Adam, my multimajor buddy, has transformed the two-year-junior-college experience into three years.

Although the prolific and varied number of classes on Adam's transcript may never fit an existing degree plan at any university without the loss of a few hours of credit, at least he's taking them at a tuition cost of approximately $1,000 a year instead of the $9,000 he would pay at some private universities. Junior college has allowed him to experiment with his major without putting him into debt for the rest of his life.

"I think you're trying to turn TJC into a four-year university, Adam," I joked.

"When do you have to apply?" Adam asked, glancing at the pile of catalogues, degree plans, and applications in front of me.

"The deadline is about six months before I want to transfer. If I apply earlier, I just have to reapply before the semester when I want to go," I reeled off, easily dispensing this information since I had repeated it to my parents so many times. "I just can't decide if I want to transfer this coming fall or spend one more year at TJC."

I gave up my internal transfer debate for a moment and leaned back in my chair to survey my community college. A gaggle of football players and sorority members drifted noisily through the student center. Just like any senior college, TJC has the full array of extracurricular activities—sports, a Greek system, honor societies such as Phi Theta Kappa, cheerleading, drill team, and choir. These activities provide an alternative way to unify the students in the absence of dorm life. For commuters, getting involved in on-campus activities means the difference between just going to school and home and getting the "full college experience." Looking at the clock, I realized my academic life would be in jeopardy if I didn't hurry to Spanish.

"¿Qué hora es?" Señor asked rhetorically, tapping his watch as I walked into the room. Although I've had one or two part-time teachers who would often walk into class ten minutes late, littering papers out of an overstuffed briefcase, punctuality and attendance matter at many junior colleges. At TJC, instructors take attendance the first few weeks of class, and students who are habitually absent may find an "advisory" letter at their permanent address or may eventually be dropped from class. For some, this seems like a flashback to high school, but it shows the personal interest many junior-college instructors take in their students.

Few instructors seem to be casual about time or teaching. From an Iranian native and Fulbright scholar who teaches American government, to a blind professor who writes the weather report for the local newspaper and radio stations (and once led me to a classroom when I couldn't find it), instructors rely on their own experience and education rather than on teaching assistants. I appreciate this hands-on approach, but today as I try to decide if I'm going or coming I would gladly trade Señor for a slightly less imposing teaching assistant.

After my boring half-hour trek to my parents' house, where I still live, my mother watched me drag myself through the door, staring at the dark circles under my eyes. "You really need to get to bed earlier. I know you had to stay up late studying this week, but you are going to wear out." She certainly meant well, but I had taken about all the friendly advice about my college career I could handle. "Look, if I had gone off to college you would have no idea what time I went to bed!"

The wrinkle between her eyes said something like, "And I wouldn't have known to wash your clothes, or help proofread that term paper, or lend you money, or . . ."

While feeling bad for snapping at my mom, I started getting dressed to drive back to town to meet friends. Junior-college towns don't usually boast the same number of clubs and live-music venues as do four-year universities, so sometimes we had to create our own social scene. After games and popular on-campus activities like homecoming or a performance, we usually wound up at IHOP late at night—sometimes followed by a trip to the bowling alley across the street. Although junior colleges attract many older students, there are plenty of "youngsters" to hang around with on weekend nights.

After a group of friends met on this particular Friday, our talk turned to some of the new but familiar faces we had been seeing during spring semester.

"Half of my high-school friends who went off to school last semester ended up coming back here," Adam said.

One of the TJC cheerleaders interrupted him and turned

to me. "Speaking of that, do you know a girl named Karen? She's going out with my brother and said she knew you."

"Sure, she's at the University of Texas."

"Not for long." The girl flicked her hair and continued. "Supposedly, she's really homesick and is transferring back here in the winter."

"Maybe you could buy her UT Austin sweatshirts," said Adam, smirking.

His words stuck in my head. Somewhere between my talking about transferring and my sifting through all the transfer materials, I realized that I was already getting something very valuable at a good price. I will transfer, but not this year. When I do, I'll get my own new college sweatshirt. One that fits me perfectly.

Carla Bass graduated from community college and is now completing a degree in journalism at the University of Texas at Austin.

the religious college

In the following essay, Kristyn Kusek enlightens us on whether you need to be a good Christian to thrive at a religious college.

A "Higher" Education

by Kristyn Kusek

When I drive the eight hours it takes me to get home from college, I pray to God: "Please don't let my car break down." During the week I'm supposed to get my period, I pray to God: "Please don't let me be pregnant." When I get stressed out about a paper on the metaphysical repercussions of neoclassism on seventeenth-century American society, I pray to God: "Please let me get through this." That is, more or less, the extent of my religious activity. I was brought up in a family that steps inside a church only on Christmas and Easter. Although I was baptized and confirmed a Catholic, I do not consider myself a member of that religion. Yet I am a senior at Holy Cross.

When I was looking at colleges, I went a little overboard and applied to thirteen schools all over the country. I wanted to attend a small school where I would get a lot of attention from professors and where I could really make myself part of the campus as Kristyn and not as number 1,238 in the Class of 1996. After I made countless visits to what seemed like a blur of campuses, my decision came down to two schools: Holy Cross, the Catholic college my father attended, and Vanderbilt, where I heard you had to dress up and have a date for football games. The idea of wearing stockings and heels to a tailgate wasn't my idea of a good time, and I preferred the ski slopes of Massachusetts to the humidity of Tennessee. After spending a Sunday locked in my bedroom making lists of pros and cons, I picked Holy Cross. There was something about the familyish feeling to the campus I liked. I now believe that this feeling stems from its Jesuit ties and the Church's mission in service toward others. Holy Cross was the only college where I saw students patiently holding doors open for people who were walking what seemed like miles behind them.

When I started telling people that I was going to Holy Cross, I got bombarded with curious questions. "Is it all girls? Do you have to wear a uniform? Are you required to go to Mass? I never knew you were religious." Holy Cross is coed, my "uniform" consists of a pair of jeans that (to my mother's disgust) could probably walk on their own since I rarely have time or the quarters to do laundry once a week, and I've been to church fewer times in my three and a half years here than I can count on one hand.

Yet there are subtle differences between a Catholic college and, say, a state school. For instance, I come from a moderately racially mixed area in northern Virginia and my friends in public high school were named Tarek, Genevieve, and Thao. My friends at Holy Cross have names like Mary Catherine and John Paul. Most of them went to private Catholic schools all their lives, and most are at least half Irish. White, upper-middle-class kids are the bulk of the student body.

My French class my first year was taught by a Jesuit priest. I've never had to be in the same room as a priest for three days a week (much less graded by one), and I was initially a little nervous that my performance would be judged by his perception of me as a Christian rather than as a student. Religion is part of the college's core curriculum, but the courses don't focus solely on Catholicism. The class I took to fulfill the religion requirement focused on Buddhism, Hinduism, and Moslem religions. Oddly, the only times I felt out of place for not being a Catholic were in classes that had nothing to do with religion. Occasionally, a story from the Bible would come up in an English class and while other students (whose education was solely of the Catholic persuasion) could remember the story from an elementary-school religion class, I was at a loss.

The campus is dotted with religious symbols that you wouldn't find on a state school's lawn. The most obvious one is a sculpture that scared the hell out of me when I was a little girl and we'd visit my dad's alma mater. In front of the library stands the H.O.C.—a huge sculpture of the crucified hand of Christ, nail through the palm and all. A friend of mine used to climb on it late at night when she was drunk, and I've rubbed it, jokingly, for good luck. Atop the hill on which the school was built stands one of the most spectacular buildings on campus: the Jesuit residence. It looks more like a mansion than a residence, and the mouth-watering smells that waft out at dinnertime make me wonder if the priests took the required oath of poverty when they were ordained.

Our school is one of the few institutions in the country in which the president must be a priest—in other words, always a man, and most often an elderly man. Like this rule, there are plenty of traditions at Holy Cross that stem from its Catholicism. The one unbiased assumption I can make about my school is that traditions die hard here.

I am a liberal-minded gal and I started calling myself a feminist before I knew what the word meant. My belief system doesn't exactly jibe with the school's unwritten rules. For instance, since Holy Cross is a Catholic school, you cannot get birth control on campus. In fact, you cannot even ask the campus infirmary questions about birth control. My best friend at school wanted to go on the Pill and decided (or had no other option) to go to Planned Parenthood to get a prescription. One year later, she went back to the clinic to get a new prescription. The parking lot in front of the building was filled with anti-abortion protesters, and my friend did not feel safe going to the clinic that morning. She didn't know how to explain that she is Catholic, pro-life, and on the Pill. She didn't pull into the parking lot. The Holy Cross sticker on the rear window of her car felt, to her, like a brand. Today, we go to the clinic together to get the pills. When she stops the car in front of the building, she rolls down the back window so the sticker doesn't show.

Our campus is also not known for its compassion toward homosexuality. I believe homophobia exists on any campus, since colleges are essentially microcosms of our society, but some of the administration's actions at my school have shocked me. Last year, a woman in my class "came out" publicly to the college in a lecture in which she discussed the difficulty of being a lesbian at Holy Cross. Just a few weeks ago, the gay-support group (provided through the chaplain's office) wanted to invite Wilson Cruz, "Ricky," the gay teen on *My So-Called Life*, to speak. The administration said he couldn't come. Eventually, after a lot of pushing and pulling, he was allowed to come on the condition that the group invite a Catholic gay speaker next. The school is slowly becoming more accepting. And the main thing I remember from that lecture about homosexuality at Holy Cross was the action of a priest who has been at the college since the 1930s; he stood up during question-and-answer period and asked the audience to applaud the student's speech.

Women's studies has become, for me, a buffer to the conservative atmosphere here. Although the Women's Forum (our feminist group on campus) is occasionally ridiculed for passing out condoms on the steps of the campus center (imagine?) or picketing speakers like Clarence Thomas (a "respected" alum of the school), there is definitely a strong group of women on this campus. My involvement with women's studies at Holy Cross has changed my feminism in a way that I don't think would happen anywhere else. While I am avidly pro-choice, some of the feminists I know are pro-life. I don't agree with the Catholic Church that women can't be priests, yet some feminists I know go to Mass every Sunday and say the rosary. I know of only one women's-studies professor who is definitely Catholic. So I wouldn't say that the women's-studies program is defined by a "Catholic feminism." Rather, the program encourages a lot of different beliefs.

Being female and liberal at Holy Cross isn't easy, but it hasn't made me miserable either. With only two months to go until graduation, I can't say that I wouldn't do it all over again. Women have been at this school for twenty-four years and women's studies has existed for only five years; there is a "new tradition" growing here. Most of the people I know aren't die-hard Bible beaters. This school, because of its size, is often characterized as a family. And, like any family, it can be dysfunctional. Even so, when I graduate, I know I'll be back to visit Holy Cross, if only to slap the H.O.C. five.

Kristyn Kusek graduated in 1996 and is now an editorial assistant at Glamour *magazine.*

the military college

The last several years have been filled with reports on women at military colleges. From the news we've learned that not all military academies create environments in which female cadets feel welcome. A 1995 survey conducted by the General Accounting Office found that female cadets at West Point, the Naval Academy, and the Air Force Academy were experiencing sexual harassment at the same and in some cases at higher rates than four years ago. It found that approximately 95 percent of academy women experienced at least one form of sexual harassment in the 1991 academic year. It also noted that many women felt there was no improvement in the atmosphere for reporting sexual harassment and continued to fear reprisals from male students and commanders if they did report incidents.

However, despite sometimes hostile conditions, women cadets have perservered and are succeeding in the military. In 1995, for the first time in the United States Military Academy's 193-year history, a woman, Second Lieutenant Rebecca Marrier, took the number-one class rank, an honor bestowed upon the graduating cadet who best represents the academy in three programs: military, academic, and physical.

If you plan to pursue a career in the military, investigate your options closely and go with the one which will best ensure your success. But first do some basic research by reading the next essay; Tara Jo Osburn will tell you what only a woman in the military knows.

The Few and the Proud

by Tara Jo Osburn

With the intense yelling and the banging of trash cans, I suddenly realized my sleepless night had not been just a bad dream. I leaped from my bed and quickly put on my gym gear and tennis shoes. I moved as if in a daze, motivated more by fear than by anything else. I entered the hall and followed fifty other identically dressed company mates outside. Not a word was spoken except for those shouted by the drill instructors. We ran out to the giant lawn and lined up for calisthenics. Not until this July morning in New York had I realized how cold and dark it was at 5 a.m.

Since grade school, I had always dreamed of following in the footsteps of my only brother. Exciting stories of his life in the military were commonplace in my family throughout my junior high and high school years. He graduated from the Air Force Academy in 1990 and went on to become a pilot in the U.S. Air Force. I chose a different route, one by sea rather than by air. I graduated from high school, packed my bags, and set out for the United States Merchant Marine Academy, also known as Kings Point.

The initial shock set in when I realized I was thousands

of miles from the small Montana town where I had lived all my life. And although I knew I had their complete love and support, my family and friends seemed to be worlds away. Not only was I surrounded by strangers, but I was now a minority; men outnumbered women ten to one. I truly was "a woman in a man's world." Kings Point was the first federal academy to admit women, but even today there are some old salty dogs who still believe that women have no place being out on ships or at the academy being trained to sail them. I had to perform as well as, if not better than, my male counterparts just to prove to them that I had the right to be here.

Throughout our four years at the academy, we are expected to meet the same standards as the guys, both physically and mentally. When it came to morning physical training, I was fortunate to have drill instructors who usually chose women to lead the company during runs. This did single us out, but it also allowed everyone to start and finish together, because we set the pace. And while we were slowing down some of the guys, we were just as fast as, if not faster than, the others. This is just one way that the school stresses unity, both within the class and in the individual companies. Even then, we realized how important it was to help one another make it through this place.

Unity was emphasized regimentally, but it was obvious that things would not be that simple on a more personal basis. The girls just did not mix with the guys as well as they did with one another. During intramurals in the afternoons, the guys quickly became buddies in the relaxed atmosphere, and we stood to the side and tried our best to fit in. Sometimes a few of the men would separate from the crowd and talk with us, but not always. Even though we were supposed to be a team, competition between the sexes still existed. Not for all, but for some, having women accomplish the same things the men did tarnished the masculine image of the tough life at a military academy. Because of this, the girls grew closer together, which planted the seeds of enduring friendships.

As time went by, the barriers between us slowly eased. Our differences diminished as the routine of daily life at the academy gave everyone more things in common. No longer did gender define us, as much as did our individual personalities. The classes were small and this allowed everyone to get to know one another better. In a class of twenty, there were usually one or two other girls. This was awkward in the beginning and I was afraid that all the guys would be smarter than I was, but I adjusted and soon it was a pleasant surprise when they came to *me* for help.

Even as we grew more comfortable around each other, there was still one major cause for our lack of self-assurance. I had always heard that you never appreciate what you have until it's gone, and that held true for my hair. It had taken years to grow it out long, and only moments to chop it all off. Outside the barbershop that first day, the women were formed into one line and the men into another. Regardless of sex, there was a feeling of anxiety and uncertainty among all. There was no chitchatting, nor would it have been allowed. We were all shuffled through the barbershop like cars through a toll booth. The men got their heads shaved, and the way the barbers butchered our hair, we may as well have been shaved, too. I was traumatized. People had often told me that I look a lot like my brother, and after that haircut I could have been mistaken for him. It was as if we had been stripped of our identity. The combination of our hair, or lack thereof, and our unflattering uniforms made it very difficult to feel good about ourselves.

The very first time I went off campus I was with the crew team, of which I was then a member. My roommate and I went into a convenience store to use the rest room. As we were about to walk in, a man called out to us: "Hey! That's the ladies' room . . ." We turned and he cut his sentence short and apologized. But we went in and cried; neither of us had ever been so humiliated. After that initial butchering, we were allowed to grow out our hair on the condition that it was worn above the collar while we were in uniform. Pinning my hair into a french braid eventually became part of my daily routine. And to this day, I swear I will never have short hair again.

My class did not earn the privilege of weekend liberty until seven months after our arrival at the academy. I often thought about my high school friends partying it up at college while I spent Friday nights cleaning and scrubbing toilets for Saturday-morning inspections. When we were finally allowed to go out, everyone headed into the city to go to the bars and clubs. My girlfriends and I assumed we'd go along with the guys, since we'd become good friends after all we had been through. It no longer fazed me to be called "one of the guys," or at least that's how I felt. So I will never forget when one of my friends told me that he preferred that I did not go with them. I was shocked. He said he would feel obligated to look out for me, as he would a little sister. It was nice to hear how much he cared, but it made me angry that he didn't think I could look out for myself. And I'm positive he neglected to tell me the rest of the reason: they were worried that our presence would threaten their status as eligible bachelors. They would rather pick up women than hang out with us.

My friends back home think I must have the best social life while going to a school with so many guys. It is hard to explain how they act when they are always together with so few girls around. At first, I couldn't believe how they talked about their weekend excursions and the "chicks" they hooked up with. I used to wish that their girlfriends or mothers could see how crude the boys could be. Now that I am a senior, I realize that their level of maturity was the reason for their obnoxious behavior. I guess that is what can be expected from a group of guys who have just graduated from high school. It is not that all of us girls were pillars of maturity either, but we did deal with situations differently. I can definitely say that academy life has taught me a lot about how the male mind operates and how it matures. As seniors, we all, men and women, appreciate going out together as friends.

Most guys here at the academy have girlfriends back home or nearby. And yes, Kings Pointers do date each other, although it can be a strenuous atmosphere for relationships. Since the academy is so small, about 800 students, rumors run wild. I used to think my high school of 150 was bad, until I came here. I have not felt a sense of privacy since I left home almost four years ago. There are fewer than a hundred girls, so our social lives are often in the spotlight. Additionally, all relationships must be maintained at a professional level while we are on campus. Things that happen at college could get you kicked out of the academy. Even something as minor as holding hands is not allowed.

Life here is very strict; there are many rules which we must abide by. Although some have good intent, there are others that seem simply ridiculous. Nevertheless, I would not trade this experience for anything. The academy has opened my eyes to a world I would never have known otherwise. At the age of twenty-one, I have already spent one year of my life sailing around the world. I have visited such places as Japan,

Korea, Taiwan, Hong Kong, Guam, Hawaii, and Alaska. I have experienced the cultures of foreign countries and seen the beauty of sunsets in the middle of the Pacific. I have taken the wheel of a 50,000-ton ship worth millions of dollars. Upon graduation, I will be a licensed officer in the U.S. Navy Reserve with a Coast Guard third mate's license and a bachelor of science degree in marine transportation. The structured living and learning environment of the academy has given me, above all, the skills and the confidence to get things done and do them well.

I am proud of the things that I have accomplished, and even more so because I am a woman. At times it is difficult to be a woman in a predominately male environment, but this reflects the industry I will enter upon graduation. Had I not grown accustomed to these circumstances at school, I would have had a very difficult time stepping aboard a ship with a crew of twenty men. I have learned that it is not what you are but what you can do that matters. Obviously, men and women have particular capabilities, but it is not so much the strength of our bodies that defines our limits as it is that of our minds. I have no doubt of what I can do, even when the drill instructors scream: *"Get down on your face and give me twenty!!!"*

Tara Jo Osburn graduated in 1996 and is now a cargo coordinator for an international shipping company in New Orleans.

12 the
college in transition

In the 1980s, many of the nation's women's colleges, and some all-male colleges, went coed. In the following essay, Jenn Crowell shows us what it's like when boys join the girls' club.

Trying Not to Forget

by Jenn Crowell

When I applied to Goucher College, I thought, perhaps naïvely, that its male-female ratio would provide me with the best of both worlds. I had, after some deliberation, rejected the idea of applying to an all-women's college, since for years I'd thought of college as my mature-male mecca. At the same time, however, the ardent feminist in me demanded a college sensitive to women's needs. With women outnumbering men roughly three to one, Goucher sounded like heaven. And while my experience has been overwhelmingly positive, I must say that living at a school which hasn't quite completed the transition from single-sex to coed has its complexities.

Recently, a group of Goucher women and I sat relaxing at a Thai restaurant, trading the usual gossip and invariably getting onto the subject of the opposite sex. Someone launched a complaint about "Goucher guys," and I, being in the throes of a then-wonderful relationship with one of those guys, spluttered an objection.

"Okay, okay, let's clarify," Suzanne said. "We know there are a few atypical cases on campus, but think about the Goucher male population in general." At that point, the entire dinner table—myself included—burst into peals of laughter.

I don't want to be harsh, but as I wrote in a letter to my friend Mike in Louisiana: "A lot of men here, sadly enough, have an 'I'm-at-a-chick-smorgasbord-and-can-load-up-my-plate' mentality." Insecurity at being a campus minority, coupled with an oftentimes macho attitude, afflicts many men at Goucher, who, after spending their senior year of high school bragging about the fine situation into which they were entering, eventually realize that the college is not a *Playboy* mansion and that most women come to Goucher for its female majority and women's-college past.

On the other hand, I've found that many Goucher women have a virulent disdain for the minority of men they live among; it's way more cool for women to look elsewhere, such as Johns Hopkins or the Naval Academy in Annapolis, for their romantic encounters. Yet there's also a general wish for a slightly more numerous male population. Goucher women want men here, and better ones. So, although a lot of men and women choose Goucher for the same reason, because it's a predominately female school, they have totally opposite expectations of what this situation will provide.

While some men ease into the environment and establish meaningful friendships with women, others have more difficulty dealing with their new minority status.

One example of this is the Ms. Goucher Pageant, in which men stage a mock beauty pageant and dress up as female contestants. This has been an annual source of controversy on campus, with the men defending it as a way to ridicule such pageants, and women protesting that it is filled with sexual innuendos and sex stereotypes meant to insult the female majority.

Still, Goucher is not a hotbed of misogyny and sexism, the way some larger universities are, and not only because the female population is larger. There are no fraternities on campus, and the administration generally acts with sensitivity and tact in handling the transition (such as enforcing a rigorous sexual-assault policy, and maintaining a well-developed women's-studies department). The faculty is also roughly even in terms of male-female ratio, an unusual vestige of its women's-college days, which provides a balanced perspective in the classroom. I've taken courses in which there have been only two males (namely, women's studies, a fact telling in and of itself!) and courses in which equal numbers of men and women have been present, and I've noticed no difference in the dynamics; all students at Goucher tend to be opinionated, but in my experience men don't dominate classes any more than women do.

It's in the athletic, extracurricular, and social spheres, and in the general mind-set of the campus, that the pitfalls of Goucher's transition occur. For example, I was selling T-shirts and other WIG items at Goucher's celebration of twenty years of women's studies this past fall, and a female student from one of my classes came up to the WIG president and me and said that she was interested in working with us but she was "afraid to be labeled a feminist." And while Goucher has long been known as a strong supporter of women's sports, Goucher's male athletic teams' events are much better publicized and better attended than those of the women's teams, and events put on by the women's-studies department suffer from a serious lack of student attendance. Even a few men can change the consciousness of a whole environment, an environment which, in Goucher's case, was once known to embrace feminist concerns. Now a different type of woman is attending the school than when it was single-sex. She is more middle-of-the-road, wanting a women's-college environment while having men around, wanting a feminism which gives men some slack.

Even though many Goucher students don't participate actively in lectures about women's issues, the majority of students participate passively. All the changes that are taking place while Goucher becomes more coed are discussed regularly within many informal groups over lunch, in the campus newspaper, in classes, and in dorms. It is a rare environment in which women's issues are spoken about freely by members of both sexes regularly. And because of this, the college enters into its coed existence with the strength of its single-sex past. For me, the world at Goucher is a good one, for as the school I attend redefines itself and realizes its complexities, so do I.

Jenn Crowell is a sophomore at Goucher and author of the novel Necessary Madness.

Three

The

Social

Scene

13

liberal
or conservative

The political climate of a college can affect every part of your college experience. Whether a campus is conservative, liberal, middle-of-the-road, or plain apathetic will determine who will be your classmates, what you will learn, how you will party, and even what you will eat. It's important to choose a college where your values and beliefs can be comfortably expressed, where you can be challenged without being silenced.

In the following essays, Thea Joselow explains why sometimes crunchy can be hard to swallow, and Sara Peterson shows us the new old school.

Crunchy

by Thea Joselow

the choice to attend Oberlin College was one of the most irresponsible decisions I have ever made. Not that there was anything wrong with the decision, but the method involved in reaching it had more to do with flipping a coin than with the careful weighing of options. For some reason, I had always wanted to go there; it probably had something to do with the name, since I didn't know much about the place until I had already applied. Everyone said it was a great school, with cool people, good classes, and more than its share of fun. It seemed like a good idea at the time, and it turned out to be absolutely wonderful. As a serial transfer student (three colleges in two years), I was relieved finally, albeit accidentally, to find a school where I felt I had a place.

Of course, life at a notoriously liberal college is not necessarily easy. It is not always granola and the Grateful Dead. People sometimes define themselves by their particular chosen issue. Coed dorms, coed bathrooms, coed rooms sometimes, extracurricular groups and activities for just about anything you can name, constant scandal and every possible configuration of clothing are a few of the defining things that I think of as part of living on a liberal campus. However, the main defining characteristic of a liberal versus otherwise campus is the degree of respect that is necessary to maintain and preserve that environment. You will learn to respect, if not agree with, people who hate men, who hate meat, who hug trees, who just want to subvert the dominant paradigm in any way they possibly can. Everyone has to work to accommodate one another, every life-style, and every conceivable dietary variation.

There is virtually no such thing as an average day in the life of any student, but this holds particularly true on one of the more liberal campuses. Every day can be atypical in its own special way. I chose to live in one of the co-ops my junior year. The student co-op association, which is student-owned and run, rents buildings from the college and we all work together to feed, house, and govern about six hundred college students. As a co-op, we are all supposed to cooperate, which is not always an easy task when you're dealing with hundreds of eighteen- to twenty-two-year-olds. For example, I woke up in my co-op this morning, went to the kitchen, and found an announcement that we were going to have lactose elections during dinner. There were a couple of lactose-intolerant people and one vegan who found our current policy (namely: Lactose? You got a problem with lactose? Can someone tell me exactly what constitutes lactose?) inadequate.

On the way to class, I walked by people standing around tables expounding environmental issues, some avid animal-rights supporters passing around petitions, and a slew of sidewalk chalkings supporting gay rights and denouncing homophobia, homo-avoidance, and homo-ignorance. By this point, I was more socially aware than the despicably early hour and my lone cup of coffee would have you believe.

At lunch, I pushed aside a handful of leaflets protesting against the meat industry and the objectification of women, to make enough room for my garden burger, locally grown salad, and recycled napkins. My friends and I discussed how there is a word for everything and terminology for every variation on every possible life-style. Our prime examples were the different words used for various sexual preferences; there's heterosexual, bisexual, questioning, omnisexual, asexual, and (my personal favorite) hetero-flexible.

First-year students sometimes seem intimidated by this charged atmosphere. No one wants to proclaim his or her ignorance of an issue or sound uninformed. First-years sometimes walk past the tables of protest because it is a little overwhelming; juniors or seniors walk on by because they already know about it, decline to comment, are too busy, or have decided that they're not interested. You don't have to know where you stand on every issue, you don't even have to be aware of every issue. But curiosity and diplomacy are strongly recommended.

When lunch is over, Emily takes off to go to work at the sex-information center, to counsel people on any number of things; Sarah wanders off to meet a professor for coffee; Anna heads for the library to study, sleep, and surf the Net. I have to go to a class where we split into groups and engage in Afro-centric, politico-centric, feminist, and Marxist interpretations of the same short story, to demonstrate how the schema you bring to a situation changes the entire meaning.

One of the things that I found really surprising is that, for all the craziness and partying that goes on (and there are some wild parties in a place where the only thing you really know how to do is be exactly yourself), people do generally take their education very seriously. My classes tend to be seminars taught by professors who are truly interested in both the subject and the student. Lectures are interrupted by questions, discussions, and arguments. Professors are not so much trying to convert you to a particular ideology as they are trying to teach you how to think, draw your own conclusions, and defend them. We therefore write a lot of papers.

Also, there seems to be more drinking and more drugs than at some other colleges. But really, since we don't sneak around as much, what's there is more obvious. In recent years, there has been a lot of serious talk about the administration cracking down on alcohol and drug use. And there have been situations where the authorities were called and some students had legal difficulties, but the unofficial rule is that students should make educated decisions rather than have the administration enforce a really strict substance-abuse policy.

Even with a liberal social atmosphere, it can still get a little oppressive. Everyone's got a cause, a mission. Everyone is trying to change something, to be a little louder than his or her opponents, but the basic understanding most of us share is that along with the concept of freedom of speech there is the corresponding freedom to listen or not to listen. Some of us are selectively apathetic, subscribing to the "you can't make me care" theory. But we all seem to know when to give it a miss and just go out for a beer, coffee, or ice cream.

At dinner tonight, the co-op got into a raging fight about our lactose policy. People joked about demonstrating against lactose intolerance. We eventually agreed—a truly infuriating yet wholly fair way to make policy decisions—on a policy which stipulates that for every meal there must be a lactose-free alternative of comparable quality and nutritional content. We spent the rest of the semester fighting like rabid dogs about the specifics, but eventually we almost worked it out—for the most part, kind of.

There are some strange distinctions made in this kind of environment. A couple of people made real enemies by being relentless in their insistence on certain petty rules (e.g., failure to compost your personal leftovers is a crime punishable by one hour of forced labor cleaning the refrigerators).

I have learned that respect is the key to finding a place for yourself. I have learned patience and understanding. I have learned how to disagree with someone without holding it against him or her. I have learned how to share a bathroom with men (it is surprisingly easy) and that they can never seem to rinse out the sink after they shave. I have also learned that fifty people sharing a house, chores, and food, and living cooperatively, are bound to get on one another's nerves, that the person who has the remote control for the house TV is king; and while I've learned a lot about how to do things, I have certainly learned just as much about how not to do them.

Thea Joselow and her mother co-authored a book entitled When Divorce Hits Home.

Do the Right Wing

by Sara Peterson

i remember we—a circle of seniors—had been talking about cheap khakis, macaroni recipes, and the secrets of cable-TV splicing as we waited for our professor to arrive. She usually started class with casual, upbeat conversation. But on this particular day she walked into the classroom, smacked her papers on the lectern, and put her palm to her forehead in an attempt to press out the anger wrinkles. "My new Honda was just rear-ended," she said. Then she rattled off a few obscenities, until the guy beside me faked a throat-clearing and a few women shuffled uncomfortably in their chairs. "I'm sorry," Dr. Mitchell said. "Did that offend you?" The silence was an affirmation. After all, this is Texas Christian University—often parodied as Texas Conservative University—where many people feel that you should watch your language.

At TCU, conservatism pervades college life. No alcohol

is served at athletic events; it's rumored that the Grateful Dead once played here in the seventies, but there's been no rock concert since; letters to the editor often quote the Bible; and a heated controversy erupted one semester after an on-campus resident hung a condom grab bag on her door in consideration of her neighbors' sexual safety. Like me, most of the student body comes to TCU from the nation's conservative niche—the Southern and Midwestern states—where we were raised to believe that being conservative means being traditional, family-oriented, personally responsible, modest, and, of course, Republican. When I first visited TCU, my tour guide was a girl from Omaha. She talked like me, she dressed like me, our dads even had the same first name, and it was a comfortable feeling to know that people at college would be like people from home. It made me feel secure, it made me feel welcome, and it made me choose TCU. When I enrolled, then, I had a much smoother transition than many of my high school friends who had branched out to more liberal campuses, where individuality, they told me, was so sanctioned that they had felt very much alone, isolated and disoriented, when they first arrived. Eventually they learned to adjust to the differences, and they learned from that adjustment, but most of them endured a painful freshman year. I admired them for the courage it took to go someplace different.

Adjusting to on-campus living was especially easy. The lounges in the all-female dorms at TCU (and there is only one small and not-so-popular coed dorm) are decorated to look like the houses we had left behind, with pastel carpet, flowery wallpaper, the kind of bright plump sofas your mother would buy, and the kind of mahogany coffee tables your father would insist upon. Paintings hang above the fireplaces, hutches are full of china, staircases wind, and baby grand pianos stand in cozy corners.

Being at a conservative school also means living with rules that more liberal schools don't have. At TCU, every dorm has the escort rule: no guys can be inside the dorm without a female escort, and all visiting males must be signed into a guest book that sits like watchful parents at the front door (and guys can only come through the front door). Men must be out by 2 a.m. on weekends and by midnight on weekdays (the 2 a.m. curfew was bumped from midnight only three years ago), and they can't come back until noon the next day. Even though the rules are rigid, the safety they provide is reassuring. From 1991 to 1994, only one sex offense was reported on campus. Plus, there's welcomed freedom in being able to walk braless in tiny pajamas in the mornings among females only.

Behind the closed doors of a dorm room (of those twenty-one and older) is the only place on campus where alcohol is allowed, but you won't find much drinking going on anyway—lawful or unlawful. And if it is unlawful drinking, the repercussions are severe: a stiff fine, mandatory alcohol counseling for even the first offense, and most likely the evil eye from those who know of your offense. In 1994, with about 5,500 undergraduates attending TCU, there were only sixty-five liquor-law violations, and only four drug violations. One of the more popular organizations on campus devotes itself entirely to promoting alternatives to drinking. As a matter of fact, some of the most popular and active students on campus belong to various religious organizations which do not allow their members to drink alcohol.

A homey, protective environment prevails throughout the campus, and not just within the dorms. Over the years, several of my professors have become quasi-mom-and-pops, calling me if they heard I was sick, meeting me in their offices for quiet conversations, even inviting me to dinner at their homes. There is a very collective feel to my university; no one could get through this college a no-namer or a loner—there are too many people who are always trying to care. And I believe this has a lot to do with the conservative, family-like atmosphere of the campus.

There are times when I think the domestic feel to my campus is a little extreme. For example, I see a lot of men and women in an awful rush to find love, involve themselves in long-term relationships, and get engaged. Even after four years here, I am still shocked to see how many people seem to be pursuing a different kind of "diploma"—the one set in 14-karat gold, cut pear-shaped, and sometimes received as early as junior year. They also seem to be rushing into the most traditional types of marriages, where the men work and the women stay home raising babies. Incidentally, when I'm talking about love and relationships, I'm talking about heterosexual love and relationships. Homosexuality is silenced here. A gay and lesbian support organization became official only two years ago, and it still seems sadly secretive. If you want to go to a meeting, you have to call, leave a message, and someone calls you back and tells you where the meeting is going to be held, since it's never announced. During the nationwide gay and lesbian awareness week, our campus held no demonstrations or rallies, and only a few signs were posted to call attention to it. Chalked on the sidewalk next to those few signs: "Gays gave us AIDS. Go back to the closet." Fortunately, this was cleaned off immediately, as many students were furious and embarrassed.

On a lighter note, I'd like to poke a little fun at some of

the conservative fashions seen on my campus—especially women's fashion. Many women wear long skirts or dresses, full makeup, and bulbous hoop earrings—all for an average class-filled Wednesday. I'm not sure why this style has caught on. Still, when I see a woman walk into geology wearing flats and a blazer, I think "conservative." We do have our lovable granola types, trendy thrift-shop models, the "furs-are-worn-by-beautiful-animals-and-ugly-people" T-shirt wearers. There are even some people who consider themselves liberals, although they are definitely a minority.

Except for the professors. Strange as it may seem, the professors at TCU are probably the most liberal people you'll find on campus. And sometimes they are more tolerant of different opinions and views than are the students. You can see a professor's frustration take the form of a loud sigh and a red face when he or she wants to conduct an uninhibited debate in class on religion, ethics, and political strategy. But the participants are often too reserved and traditional for the professor's liking. One of the most popular and esteemed professors at TCU teaches a riveting philosophy class where students are asked questions like "Why is abortion legal?" "Should homosexuals be allowed to marry?" "Is there a God?" This professor tells his students on the first day of class, "You better leave your preconceived, conservative notions at the door when you come here, because this is, believe it or not, a *liberal*-arts college, where you should be open-minded and accepting if you ever expect to learn." It took most of us weeks to stop blushing at some of the things he said, but eventually we did learn to shed many inhibitions and reconstruct what we thought was appropriate for an afternoon discussion. Now, to tell the truth, I don't think I could forget the ideas of Kant and Descartes if I tried. Nor will I ever forget my professor's tenet that taught me how to learn, which is what any school, liberal or conservative, should claim as the highest hope for its graduates.

Over the summer, Sara Peterson interned at the Dallas Bureau of The New York Times.

14

greeks vs. independents

Joining a group of women who will provide you with support, guidance, and friendship throughout college, and even after graduation, is one of the greatest things about sorority life. It is what causes many sorority members to feel a lifelong attachment to their alma mater, so that sorority women are up to three times more likely to donate money to their schools after graduation. And the main advantage of a sorority is that it guarantees you a social life—the sisters will introduce you to the brothers, get the conversation started and the drinks pouring. But this is also where sororities get a bad rep. A recent survey found that 80 percent of women in sororities binge-drink; that is, have four or more (many times eight or ten) drinks in a row, compared to 36 percent of independent women. And while heavy drinking in the Greek system is not news, the fact that sorority members are 20 percent more likely than independent women to have had an unwanted sexual advance is. This is one reason why some women opt for the independent route. Others stay independent because they think that choosing an exclusive group of friends without getting to know them first is just weird.

If a school with a Greek system is on your list, you will eventually have to choose one of these two very different *options. Even though you don't have to make a choice until your first or sometimes your second year of college, knowing what both these choices really entail, and figuring out if you will feel comfortable in the overall environment, is something you should do now. In the following essays, Keely Schields shows us what really goes on in the sorority houses, and Jesse Souweine shows us what goes on outside them.*

The Sisterhood

by Keely Schields

"**S**o, what made *you* decide to go through rush?" asked the members of Gamma Phi, the Theta, and Tri-Delta. With the possible exception of my major, this was the question I heard most when I went through rush. At least one person from each of Kansas State's twelve sororities asked me my reasons, and although it was a common question, most of these women asked as if they were uniquely and genuinely interested in my case. In a week of small talk and pleasantries, it wasn't hard to spot such sincerity. I guess I just didn't have that sorority look. I looked sort of butch—still do—but I didn't have the courage to answer with the same degree of sincerity. What I told them was that I thought it would be a great way to make a few fast friends before classes began, which was only part of the truth.

The whole truth was that I had been bribed. If I had to do it over again, I still probably wouldn't have admitted to this. Who could ever own up to making a major life decision on something as irrelevant as $180? It was like basing a decision on the flip of a coin, or a shallow five-minute conversation, but in my case there was no better way.

Unlike my decision to go to K-State, which had been simple, even obvious, my decision to go through rush was one I agonized over. Whether or not a student joined a Greek organization at K-State was clearly a big deal. Coming from Goodland, a small town in western Kansas, I could see that pledging a house might establish an immediate base of acquaintances at this enormous university. Then again, my primary reason for going to college was to earn a degree in English; the social temptations of a sorority might affect my academic performance, and I wouldn't stand for that. Besides, was I so desperate that I would stoop to buying my friends? That's how the whole thing struck me, so I spent the summer before my freshman year trying to forget about it.

Evidently, my parents didn't forget. While we were watching TV one night in July, not long before K-State's rush application deadline, my mom asked me once and for all whether I planned on joining a sorority or not. I didn't know, I said, but the $180 rush fee seemed too high a price to find out. My dad (a charter member of the Sigma Chi chapter at Fort Hays State University) immediately offered to foot the bill, and suddenly there was nothing to lose. I might not pledge a house, but I would go through rush to satisfy my curiosity.

Rush is a good name. I remember the week as a whirlwind of fatigue, emotion, and suspense. At my first party, a girl took me inside and asked me my name, my major, where I was from, what made me decide to go through rush. Then a different girl came and asked me my name, my major, blah, blah, blah. At the next house, I had a series of strikingly similar conversations, and it started to get pretty old. I couldn't believe I was being judged on the basis of this same conversation, and I didn't know how it was supposed to help *me* reach any decisions. So I remained in a state of blissful ignorance, which I'm convinced is the best way to experience rush. The rushees who knew too much about the mechanics of the process, or details about individual houses, were uniformly disappointed. My friend Jacque, for example, was released after two days by the house to which she was a legacy through her sister. She was so upset she dropped out of rush.

Still, I hated the small talk, the wondering, and the feeling that I was being talked about (or being laughed at) when the parties were over. At the Kappa Kappa Gamma house party, I was picked by Jeri Ann, whom I knew from high school. Right away she told me it was cool if I didn't feel like talking, then she proceeded to talk my head off. I was only too happy to relax and listen for once. She was pleased I'd gone through it and stuck it out. Wherever I ended up, she said, it would become whatever I wanted it to be.

I was quite satisfied when I ended up back at the Kappa house. Not only did I know Jeri Ann, but this was the house in which I had been most at ease all week. I couldn't explain how a process as superficial and chancy as rush could work so well. It was as if Panhellenic dumped the puzzle pieces on a table, gave the bottom a good swift knee, and watched them fly. Instead of landing all askew, though, the majority somehow managed to fall into place.

There was no fast and easy way of knowing what any of my new sisters were like. As in any other relationship, it took time. We paid our membership fees, but we still had to earn each other's trust. And while I love the continual process of connecting with my sisters, it hasn't all been warm and fuzzy. I now live in a house with sixty-seven other women, most of whom do not share my sleeping and waking schedule, and some of whom I don't even like. The second semester of our sophomore year, for example, my friend Kristen and I had to share a bedroom with two people we couldn't stand, and the feeling was mutual. One night, when we were absolutely fed up, Kristen and I drove out to the Tuttle Creek dam and cussed a blue streak, swearing up and down that we would quit. When we were a little less incensed, the two of us would simply go for coffee and talk things over. That's how our nightmare semester turned into the best ever.

From the very beginning, the sorority offered my pledge class some old-fashioned encouragement to meet (primarily fraternity) men. By old-fashioned, I mean that, rather than being given handy tips on picking up guys or something of that nature, we were gently propelled into the paths of men. After we had been pledges for about a week, our pledge trainer and her committee rounded us up and took us to a mixer for the new pledges of all of K-State's fraternities and sororities. With a familiar face never far away and with my chitchat skills recently sharpened through rush, I experienced added confidence in striking up conversations in this exciting vast new sea of men.

In fact, I managed to find a date for our first party at this mixer, and he subsequently invited me to his fraternity's first party. The various theme parties, functions, and formal dances a Greek organization holds over the course of a semester offer an opportunity for more formal social interaction, which is lacking outside of the Greek system. I've always found them to be a nice change from putting on jeans and going out on a solo date or to an apartment party. In the case of my sorority's parties, I've also learned the responsibility of graciously entertaining someone for an entire evening.

Officially, Kappa Kappa Gamma does not condone drinking for any member under the age of twenty-one; in other words, the majority of pledge and active members. Officers frequently remind everyone of this policy. Unofficially, however, there is a fraternity party taking place somewhere at any given moment, and the guys throwing it have alcohol, and they would love to share it with women. Most of the women who show up to do so are members of sororities, due to the sheer connectedness of the Greek community. One sorority woman finds out about a party from a friend in a fraternity, and before you know it, the bulk of her house is hip to it. Hence, underage women in sororities probably meet with greater opportunity to drink than do their independent counterparts. I can scarcely recall a time when the opportunity wasn't there, but I can recall several occasions when I said a simple "no, not tonight." I attribute my ability to say no to the ease with which it was accepted, as well as to the sorority's emphasis on academics and moral standards.

I remember most vividly the first fraternity party I ever went to. After Bid Day, a couple of girls from my rush floor came to my dorm room and invited me to come with them to a party at a fraternity house where they knew some guys. So I went. As we walked up to the house, the guys on the porch stood up and waved. The first thing I saw as we climbed the steps was a huge trash can from which one of the guys pulled a dripping-wet beer and asked if we would like one. Sure, we did. Then one of the guys my friend knew took us inside for a tour. We climbed the first flight of stairs to a hallway lined with bedrooms. The hall was filled with girls, smiling and sipping from their beers as they talked with their hosts. We walked past a bathroom with open showers that reminded me of my high school locker room, and I suddenly realized that guys, lots of them, actually lived here. Several very good stereos were competing with one another.

Beer. Girls. Buddies. Bedrooms. After a year of regular attendance at parties more or less like this first one, it would strike me that the sheer proximity of all these things was rather convenient. Everything was right there for those guys. Why go out? But it didn't strike me that night. I ended up in a bedroom with about twelve other people, playing a drinking game. My friends and I didn't stumble home to the dorms until four in the morning.

Drinking and partying are not the only reasons Greek organizations are considered morally questionable. For example, when I glance around the formal living room at an all-house meeting, the only women of color I see are one Asian-American and two Hispanic women. Although this exclusion—racial, ethnic, and otherwise—is no longer intentional or desirable, it becomes immediately obvious each year that too little effort has been made to get minority women to go through rush in the first place.

Now that I have been three times on the other side of rush, I do know what a sorority is looking for in a pledge. We are looking for someone whose high school grades indicate the potential for academic success at the university level. It isn't only that we pride ourselves on academic excellence; if most of the pledge class flunked out, the house would go under financially. Because we want members who will contribute to the house, we are looking for pledges who were highly involved in extracurricular activities in high school. In addition, we are looking for pledges who maintain high moral standards.

It's an unfortunate fact of life that people who are outgoing and/or physically attractive have a huge advantage as far as first impressions are concerned. Initially, these are the rushees who appeal most to the rushers. I think our saving grace is that every active member tends to stand up for the kind of rushee she was. In my own case, I would never allow a shy girl to be released on that basis, nor would most of us allow a girl to be released on the basis of looks, as most of us fall something short of beautiful ourselves.

Once we have our new pledges, all that is asked of them is that they get to know the house. This includes getting to know other members, as well as the history and ritual. The best way to do this is to participate in house meetings and social activities. I can honestly say that, to my knowledge, my sorority has never made me or any other member the victim of mental or physical abuse. Nor do I believe that the members of any of K-State's other sororities have been subjected to anything that can be construed as hazing.

Outside of the workings of the house itself, there are always the image-related concerns a sorority member must deal with. As an English major, I've had to make a special effort not to let it be known that I'm a member of a sorority, or else I'd be dismissed as some shallow bimbo. This is the kind of stereotype many people apply to sororities, and not without reason. I know plenty of women who are snobbish, talk perpetually in questions, and are in college only to catch a man. However, not all of them are in sororities.

What people who look down their noses at sororities don't realize is that these groups provide one of the few settings in which women come together and support one another. Sorority, literally "sisterhood," is what all women have when they come together for a common purpose. It's not chapter meetings, or symbols, or ritual. It's Becky, Lori, and I sitting by ourselves on the front steps of a fraternity house, sharing a cigar. It's nine women talking for three hours in a tiny kitchen when eight of them had only meant to say hello and pass through.

Of course, sorority can be achieved without Greek letters, so what's the point in the organized form? It's the most natural tendency in little girls, but somewhere along the road to becoming women, we seem to lose track of it. Sometimes it takes the formal encouragement of two or three Greek letters for us to find it again. I suppose it's no sillier than my deciding to rush because of a small bribe. Joining a formal Greek letter sorority has taught me to connect with a diverse group of women, many of whom I wouldn't have known otherwise. At the end of the day, they're the ones I come crawling back to, and they've been the single most significant part of my college experience. Beyond my own chapter of Kappa Kappa Gamma and my undergraduate years at K-State, I've been connected with a larger group of women nationwide for the rest of my life.

Keely Schields writes a weekly opinion column for Kansas State's campus paper, The Kansas State Collegian.

A Declaration of Independence

by Jesse Souweine

"**d**o you want to swim naked in the gorges? Because that's what Cornell is about, and we did it all the time."

As I chewed my pesto and sun-dried-tomato pizza, my gut reaction was yes: I want to swim naked whenever I can, and I want to meet witty, intelligent, motivated people just like you. The thirty-year-old bearded San Francisco lawyer who sat across from me, grilling me on my personal swimming habits, was a friend of my aunt's from her hippie, pot-smoking days at Cornell in the late seventies. To a junior in high school starting to think about my future glory days in college, swimming in the famed gorges of Ithaca, New York, sounded rebellious, a little threatening, and unquestionably appealing. All my aunt's friends told me tales of their wonderful heyday in college, living in group houses with their golden retrievers, hiking along the lush and leafy path at Buttermilk Falls, and studying Asian history, geological sciences, and the great works of Virginia Woolf, Ralph Ellison, and Zora Neale Hurston. Was there really a question that Cornell was the place for me? After two weeks in San Francisco with my aunt and her whole Cornell crew, I was convinced that, come next fall, I would no longer bear the telltale tan lines from the inhibiting bathing suits of my high school days.

"One-third of the student body at Cornell participates in the Greek system." Our blond, buff guide named something like Andrew Jefferson Walker III explained the social life to our tour group as we stood in a pack, like drowning rodents, in the drizzling Ithaca weather. He assured us that while the Greek system is very active on campus, there are myriad other social avenues down which many venture. He ticked off the gamut of extracurricular activities, ranging from the Medieval Renaissance Club that proudly kept the art of fencing alive, to the Indian Women's Dance Troupe that performed traditional dances throughout the academic year.

One-third, I thought to myself. Therefore, two-thirds of the 18,000 students are independents—that is, unaffiliated with fraternities or sororities. Fabulous. No problem. My aunt never mentioned interacting with the Greek crowd; I guess the Alpha Tau Omega boys didn't hang out with members of the Coalition to Legalize Marijuana. With such a diverse student body, I didn't anticipate befriending members of the Greek system outside of class. I wouldn't need to fall blindly into the pre-formed sororities. The tried-and-true method of meeting people and then deciding on the value of their friendship seemed like a road I felt much more comfortable taking. Before long, my jaunts through the waterfalls would be accentuated by jocular banter and intellectual discourse with my newfound non-Greek friends.

That vision, confirmed by Mr. Walker's assurances, became my spiel. Every time someone mentioned the Greek life at Cornell, it was as if I was the Chatty Cathy Doll, ready at the pull of a string to dutifully recite the magic two-thirds figure that would make it possible for me to thrive at Cornell without entering the Greek system.

By the time I slowed down enough to catch my breath, I found myself standing on the steps of Sperry Hall, filling my lungs with heavy air that still held the flavor of those lazy days of summer. I eyed the people on my floor, looking for fellow free spirits with whom I could explore the fabled gorges. But the people who occupied the cubicles, not four feet from my own, were different from what I had imagined.

"Come on, it's not like *Animal House* or *Revenge of the Nerds*. We just live together, go to some parties. It's really chill." The captain of the women's soccer team gave me and my fellow freshmen friends the lowdown on sororities as she tightened her perky ponytail. This was the first of many sorority chats during the fall of my freshman year. She enumerated some of the benefits of her sorority: Monday nights in front of the TV, intramural softball games, course advice from the older sisters, wacky theme parties. Even rush and pledging didn't sound so bad; according to my ponytailed informant, there was no discussion of family incomes at rush, and pledges weren't forced to prance among thick-necked frat boys, scantily clad and with their weight emblazoned on their forehead, as rumored. Instead, Aretha Franklin and chips with salsa welcomed the rushees, and pledging was seen as a time to bond with an older sister who mentored the Family's new addition.

From November on, rush was a constant topic of conversation, in dorms, classes, and gyms. Even I, the non-Greek advocate, found myself hoping the Brothers would proffer an invite to that week's Bash. For me and my freshmen friends, frats had the only accessible parties, since the no-drinking policy on campus was strictly enforced and few had obtained the sacred fake ID that opened the world of bars. These parties weren't nearly as awful as I had imagined; the dancing was always good and the beer was in steady supply.

Beer. Even now, I see myself in the "beer room," standing in two inches of spilled beer, being jostled by men with arms the width of my upper thigh. The panic that struck when I had no one to talk to lasted only until I finished my beer and went to refill my cup. Maybe this wasn't so bad, I thought. I could get used to this.

When the possibility of rushing came up in a call home, the emergency signal was triggered. The daily onslaught of phone calls began. "Just calling to say hi and see how you're doing," chirped my mother's or my aunt's voice on my answering machine. My mother saw her biggest fears about to be realized; by joining a sorority, I would lose the individuality she had cultivated for eighteen years and become an alcoholic.

"I know you, Jess," my aunt cajoled. "These people aren't it. They're just not what you're looking for, I know. I wouldn't be so adamant if I didn't think this was a really important decision."

"It's not so clear anymore," I told her. "Cornell is very different from what it was ten years ago." I tried to explain to her that the intellectuals who liked to party but weren't Greek had disappeared. "They left when Reagan got elected. And the drinking age is twenty-one, not eighteen; the frats are the only place for us to party."

"I know it's hard, but it takes time to find a group," she advised me. "I just don't want you to close yourself off in a sorority."

"I want to keep my options open," I explained. "I registered for rush, so I don't have to decide yet. I'm not committed, don't worry. We'll talk more when I'm home for winter break."

Winter break—who could imagine the comfort and thrill of being home. We were all back, after four months apart. The clothes were altered, the lingo changed, but the relationships with my high school friends were intact. Effortlessly, I slipped back into my old group's routine: hanging together, working out together, talking together. This is what I love about having a group, I thought, and if a sorority can do that for me, then great. What did my aunt know, anyway? I don't always have to listen to her, especially since her Cornell information was outdated, I told myself my last night at home.

I came back to school at the end of January, along with eight hundred other rush-ready freshmen. Returning to my room after a fashion consult next door about my Day 1 Rush outfit—not too formal, but definitely not jeans—I saw the red light on my machine blinking.

"Hi, this is Tammy, your Rho Chi," sang the high-pitched voice. "I'm leading your rush group and we're meeting tomorrow in front of Baker flagpole at 9 a.m. If you have any questions, feel free to call me. And don't forget, wear tights tomorrow because it's gonna be a cold one. B'bye."

Wait, what am I thinking? I can't do this. It's January in Ithaca and there's a blizzard. Does she really think I'm stupid enough to go outside with my legs covered only in a thin pair of tights? Get real.

What was it about the message? The tone of her voice? The words Rho Chi? The idea of tights? I picked up the hot-pink rush booklet I received at registration and realized that I couldn't do it. The packet didn't fit in my room, not its color or its content. I would never meet Tammy, or any other primped and proper girls who would stand in their foyers, smiling. So, as the other twenty-three women on my floor woke at the crack of dawn to prepare themselves for a long week, I pulled the covers up, switching my alarm off in my sleep.

For six days, my friends hiked all over campus, listening to sorority anthems, answering questions about their major and their favorite musical groups, and straining their cheek muscles from smiling eight hours a day. That week, I read, worked out, explored Ithaca, and waited for classes to start. The loneliness was tolerable thanks to Alison, a new "independent" friend. On the week's grand finale, bid night, I went to coffee with Alison. We bonded over our lack of Greek affiliation, but our conversation moved quickly to our interests and aspirations. Walking back to the dorm, high from the conversation and from too much caffeine, I forgot that rush was over and the chosen few had been remanded to this, that, or the other sorority of their choice, or someone else's. I went to bed feeling liberated from my momentary lapse of judgment about Greek life. I always knew it wasn't for me.

I woke up groggy, grabbed my yellow shower bucket, and unlocked the door. The fluorescent hallway light forced my pupils to shrink. Squinting, I saw the colorful poster pasted on the door across the hall: a panda, cut out of black and white construction paper. Red glitter encircled the bear like a necklace, trailing off its body to form three capital Greek letters in the palm of an outstretched paw. "Debby" was scrawled in the bubble coming out of the panda's mouth. What a welcome.

The hard spray pulsed on my head as I tried to wash the images from the hall out of my mind. Which was worse, Delta Gamma's triangle accented with streamers, Kappa's key with pledge's name stenciled in pastel letters, or Alpha Hi Omega, who used the Greek alphabet to spell the name of the new inductees. The hum of the water stopped. I stepped into my shower flops and was greeted by the piercing voices of the soon-to-be Sigma Delta Tau girls who lived on my floor.

"The bid party was soooo fun. I was completely wasted. My big sister and my big-big were totally introducing me to all the cute Alpha guys. Did you know the SDTs usually date Theta Chis? It's not like a rule or anything, I guess it's just tradition, you know?" I grimaced behind the lime-green curtain, relieved that my erasable message board was the only decoration on my door.

But as the weeks wore on and I watched my friends leave the dorm, headed for a formal or a mixer to which I wasn't invited, the panda began to piss me off. Gone was his goofy, benign smile, replaced by a taunting, even condescending smirk. He was the only witness to the Friday nights I spent in my room, reading when I wanted to be raging. This felt similar to high school, where the "cool" kids, who were a minority in number, dominated the parties for the entire school. Only, at Cornell, I was no longer a card-carrying member of the preppy/jock crowd; I felt like one of the friendless, on the outside looking in. My message board, the symbol of my independence, stared at me blankly when I came home from classes.

At the end of the semester, I signed a lease for the next year's apartment with another independent whom I'd met through Alison. I finished my exams and packed up my belongings. I stopped in front of my door with my duffel bag and looked for the last time at the panda. Fuck you, I said.

The windows assured me with their nakedness. Thank God I'm not in the living room of the Alpha Chi Omega or Pi Beta Pi, with their Martha Stewart curtains that match the carpet, the sofa, even the Sisters. This small, dimly lit apartment of sophomore year reminded me of my independence and my individuality. My self-proclaimed GDI (God Damned Independent) friends welcomed me into their equally disheveled apartments for happy hour, dinner parties, and movie marathons. My frat-party shoes, with the ring of beer residue just above the sole, were shoved in the back of the closet. I loved living in my own apartment, although, truth be told, at times I was lonely. I had lost touch with many of my now-pledged friends. The promises of uninvolvement in their houses were replaced with a frightening enthusiasm to participate. Gone was the group fun we had that semester before the rush season began.

Although I had a definite group that year, it was not what I was looking for. Their weed was killer, their jazz and reggae cool, but their shtick didn't fit. These hippie kids of investment bankers and commodities brokers retained their predecessors' philosophies from the sixties but pulled out the plastic when the cherry-red VW Rabbit needed a car phone or when the eighty-dollar brown suede pants fit just right.

Although I had made a few of those special, lifelong college friends, I began to accept that there was no present-day Cornell equivalent of my aunt's group of fabulous friends.

When I left Cornell after completing my second year, I did so with excitement; not because I had finally found my place in the town rimmed by gorges, but because I wouldn't return for an entire year. After the summer, I was on my way to Cornell's Washington, D.C., program. We quickly formed a closely knit community while living in the same building. Some of these friends were in the Greek system back in Ithaca, but in the city, that status is inconsequential. We saw the monuments, went to museums, found the best happy hours, and reveled in our absence from Cornell. I also spent a lot of time without my friends while in D.C. and I came to cherish and crave the time when I could leave work and explore by myself. I learned to feel comfortable with myself. I learned to listen to myself, and not the group, to decide what to do at a particular moment.

I returned the next fall with a sense of direction in my studies and a new sense of independence. At the same time, I was glad to see that the emphasis placed on Greek life for seniors was greatly reduced. Higher-level courses, an increased sense of self, and a look toward the future focused the light away from the social scene and onto the student. Even during my last year, I was never really part of a cohesive group. Instead, I had different friends for different activities: I lived with Kristin from D.C., saw plays with Gad from economics class, went to temple with Eytan from freshman year. My lack of a clear group afforded me many possibilities for spending my precious free time.

Given a second shot at choosing a college, I would have researched my options more carefully, instead of relying on ten-year-old information. That said, I see few reasons to persuade me that I made the wrong decision. Cornell, with its gorges and Greek system, fulfilled my life in so many ways, academically, geographically, and, with a lot of work, socially. I will leave Cornell without the pledge pin of a sorority, but I'm leaving with a clear understanding of what it means to be an Independent versus being independent (there is a difference). Being an Independent though lacking the formal rules and regulations of Greek life mirrors the Greek system, in fact. I *am* leaving with a "group," it was one that I created, bringing together people who touched my life in a substantial way, and I managed to do so independently.

Jesse Souweine spent the summer working at the Feminist Press, an independent publishing house.

15

being a black woman at a predominately white school

As you flip through college catalogues and study the percentages of students of color on various campuses, you'll see very different numbers: 9%, 33%, 18%, 1%. What do they all mean? The numbers, sometimes, signify little. The best indicators of what life will be like for a student of color at a predominately white school are the kinds of cultural groups and student services provided by the college, and how all students interact. These things differ greatly from school to school. Many colleges have organizations for students of color which serve as social and political outlets. Some schools offer cultural dorms; others integrate multicultural courses into the curriculum and have faculty from different ethnicities. Looking into these aspects of a college can give you an idea of how comfortable a place it will be.

In the following essay, Angine Harriott explains life at a predominately white school.

Finding Diversity

by Angine Harriott

*t*he highlight of my freshman year at Penn was a series of bomb threats made to residents in the DuBois College House. This residence hall is predominately black, though anyone of any race can choose to live there. And even though there are white, Latino, and Asian residents in DuBois, these threats sparked many community discussions on the voluntary separation of black students from the greater Penn community. Many students, some of them black, charged that by living in DuBois "black students were limiting their Penn experience."

This theme of separation has been predominant in my three years at Penn. Black students are accused of being separatists; we eat only with black people, we go to black parties, etc. But this is virtually impossible at Penn. I spent my first two years living in DuBois not because I wanted to be separate from the white community but because it was where I felt comfortable. After four years of high school at an all-girls white prep school, I felt it my right to live where I felt comfortable. And although I live in an off-campus apartment today, DuBois is still my home. It's a place where I can go and see a familiar face, sort of like the bar in the sitcom *Cheers*.

When I think of DuBois, I think of the late-night spade

games, Sunday dinners cooked by residents, the pictures of famous black Americans on the walls of the Multipurpose Room. Within the halls of DuBois, there are heated debates about African, Caribbean, and black cultures. The house made Penn a manageable size. When I walked into DuBois, I forgot that there are twenty thousand other people on this campus. It's a place you can return to after spending a day as just another student; it restores one's individuality. The comfort comes from knowing you are surrounded by others who understand what it's like to be black in a predominately white university.

Day in and day out, I sit in classrooms that are populated mainly with white students. I have white friends and I can relate to them, but they don't understand what it's like to stand outside at 2 a.m. in 2 degrees while the fire department makes sure there isn't a bomb in their dorm. They don't know what it's like to read weekly editorials in the student newspaper about the shortcomings of their race. They cannot relate to my experience at Penn. I am forced to explain why I chose to live where I did. They are never questioned about their decisions. It's all part of being in a predominately white community.

However, the subcommunity of blacks presents its own pressures. I think a lot of black students at Penn feel strong when they enter the classroom. They feel prepared academically and they can stand their ground. But many of the same students lose this strength in the black social arena. Many put on a show for the black community; they try to act tough, or super-smart, or militant. Some are so pro-black you wonder if they're not living in the sixties. There's a pretty good mix in the black community, but then there are those who have been excluded for a variety of reasons—for acting white, dating white, or crossing over. This situation is usually

created by an ignorant few who feel they are experts at judging what is appropriately black. Then there are black students
who, for their own personal reasons, decide that being
around other black students isn't for them. Penn students
really get caught up in limiting self-created categories.

The group that has the biggest problems in this subcommunity, however, is black women. When they first arrive,
black female freshmen are of great interest to upperclassmen.
This is one of the reasons upper-class black women treat the
freshmen women with a certain aloofness. There are very
few mixed-class female relationships among black women
on this campus. We don't communicate with each other,
because we feel threatened. My friends and I talk about the
situation all the time. My friends are juniors, and I know I
can count on them anytime. We support each other through
academic, family, and social problems. But once you establish these kinds of friends, most women don't reach out to
other women. They stay with the friends they've made. I
have acquaintances who are in other classes, but that's all
they are, acquaintances.

I guess that's one of the few expectations I had coming to
Penn that hasn't been met. It's very separate here. On weekends I'm at a predominately black fraternity party or I'm
chilling with my friends. The admissions representatives sold
me on diversity, but I found that it was up to me to make
sure I had a diverse experience once I got here. I found other
sources of diversity through my involvement in the Caribbean American Student Association and my Afro-American
Studies class. I have been fortunate enough to take Latin
American classes in history and literature. Because these classes were filled with a majority of Latin American students, I
was able to learn more about their culture both academically
and socially. Being part of a dance group has also given me

the opportunity to learn about dances from India and Asia. The groups are here, the classes are here, but they weren't going to come to me. Penn, because it prides itself on being a diverse university, provided me with the opportunity to learn about myself and engage my curiosity about other cultures.

I made a conscious effort not to get swept up into just one aspect of the college. I make sure to go to football games, participate in the Ritual Hey Day that marks the transition from junior to senior year, be on the student-activities committee as well as participating in the African dance and drum troupe. I know of people who've never been to a football game or participated in non-black activities at Penn. Their experience is no less valid than mine, but it is just as limiting as that of white, Asian, or Latina students who have never participated in events that do not focus on their culture.

I've enjoyed the classes I've taken at Penn. I like the feeling of walking down Locust Walk and being at a school which has enabled me to meet people from all over the world. I feel good when I'm on the train and I meet a Penn graduate who wants to hear about all that's changed at his or her alma mater. Because I've exposed myself to many different experiences, I know I'll leave feeling connected to my school. It just took an open mind.

Angine Harriott plans on continuing to fill her life with diversity by becoming an immigration lawyer.

16
being lesbian at an intolerant college

At this time in your life, you may or may not be sure of your sexuality. You may know but just aren't telling. You may plan on telling, but just not now. Statistics indicate that most lesbians openly acknowledge their sexuality between the ages of sixteen and nineteen. This means that if you are lesbian or bisexual, you may come out in high school. And if you don't, you will probably come out in college. Either way, it is important to look into how well a college treats its gay, lesbian, and bisexual students, because colleges differ dramatically in this regard. Many colleges have gay, lesbian, and bisexual student unions. Others, like Northwestern, actively recruit openly gay employees. Some colleges even have dorms exclusively for gay, lesbian, and bisexual students. But there are many other colleges which ignore the needs of non-hetero students and in fact create campus environments which are openly hostile.

In the next essay, Kelly Smith tells what life was like at a college which accepted her as a student but wouldn't accept her sexuality.

Getting Accepted

by Kelly Smith

*h*aving attended a small Catholic all-girl's high school, and having been quite happy with that experience, I had no reservations about spending four years at Saint Mary's, a small, all-women's Catholic liberal-arts college in northwest Indiana. The familiarity of that environment seemed reassuring to a rather overprotected only child who had never really been away from home before. The small classes and high-quality faculty were definite advantages. As an additional bonus, the University of Notre Dame was located directly across the street.

Admittedly, much of the social life at Saint Mary's revolves around nearby Notre Dame. Saint Mary's functioned as a sister school until Notre Dame went coed in the early 1970s; the two schools still maintained very close relations. It wasn't long before my new friends and I were making the ritual weekend visits to Notre Dame to attend parties in the men's residence halls as well as off campus in apartments rented by students.

During my first three years at Saint Mary's, I met plenty of guys from Notre Dame and had little trouble finding dates for formal dances. My friends and I spent a great deal of our free time discussing men and confiding in one another about our good and not so good experiences with them. Something about it felt unnatural to me, however, almost as if I were playacting in order to fit in with everyone else.

I'd had the same sort of feeling in high school, when I had actually wondered why all my friends were so crazy about the opposite sex and what was wrong with me for not sharing their attitude. At the time, I thought I just needed to find the right man. By my junior year at Saint Mary's, I had met several wonderful, good-looking guys, and still something was missing; I felt no "chemistry" with them. Yet the possibility that the right man could be a woman was an alternative I was not willing to accept.

I recall having intense crushes on other girls since the age of eleven or twelve, but I had always rationalized these away as admiration instead of acknowledging the feelings for what they really were. I had always been told that homosexuality was abnormal, disgusting, and sinful. I repressed my feelings and pushed them into the far corners of my mind. But no matter how I attempted to hide them, they wouldn't go away.

For three years of college, I suffered in silence, too afraid to reveal my feelings to anyone. Even my closest friends had no idea of the inner turmoil I was experiencing. The student body at Saint Mary's and Notre Dame is overwhelmingly white, upper-middle-class, socially and politically conservative, and, not surprisingly, Catholic; while my particular group of friends was relatively diverse and open-minded, I still feared their potential reaction if they discovered what I was hiding.

I felt completely alone in my struggle. There was no visible lesbian or bisexual presence on campus, nor was there any sort of support group, with the exception of a small underground group of students at Notre Dame whose tiny ads had appeared in the student newspaper during my sophomore year. (The ads stated, "Gay, lesbian, or bisexual? We're here for you. We can't print our name, but you know who we are," together with a P.O. address.) I had not seen any ads since my sophomore year and had no idea whether the group still existed. I had never seen or heard anything at Saint Mary's regarding where to turn or what to do if you suspected that you were lesbian or bisexual. As far as the college and the general student body seemed to be concerned, homosexuality and bisexuality were simply nonexistent and therefore of no relevance.

I remember writing in my journal that I felt my feelings were "wrong," that I hated myself for having them. Although I never actually contemplated suicide, I became severely depressed and withdrawn. Soon I began skipping classes, failing to complete homework assignments, and sleeping until late afternoon on weekdays. I seemed to have lost all motivation to function normally on a day-to-day basis.

My academic problems mounted, and I turned to the counseling center for assistance. I did not have the courage to tell them what was really bothering me. I worried (needlessly) that they might be disgusted with me or notify my family, so I gave them other possible reasons for my depression, such as conflicts at home, which were a contributing factor. I did not want to take a leave of absence from school, I feared disappointing my family, so the counseling-center staff helped me withdraw from most of my classes and made arrangements to ensure that there was no disruption in my financial aid. Since the root cause of my troubles had not been treated, however, my depression and my academic problems continued.

Just as it seemed there was nowhere for me to turn, something startling and unexpected took place. Miranda, one of my best friends and a student at Notre Dame, had become increasingly close to her new roommate, and rumors had begun circulating in her residence hall that the two of them were lesbians. I initially found this difficult to believe, since Miranda had seemed exclusively heterosexual for the two years I had known her. But as time passed, I began to suspect the rumors were indeed true. I noticed that Miranda and her roommate looked at and interacted with each other in much the same way that heterosexual couples tended to do. It seemed that they were in love! Finally, at the end of our junior year, Miranda confided in me her relationship with her roommate.

Miranda was relieved to find that I was immediately supportive of her relationship and happy that she was in love. Where others were concerned, I seemed to have surprisingly little difficulty with homosexuality; with myself, I had been unrelentingly critical. Here, finally, was an opportunity to change that.

I took a deep breath and proceeded to confide in Miranda all the feelings for other women that I had bottled up inside for so long. A great oppressive weight seemed to lift from my shoulders as I spoke. Thankfully, Miranda was just as supportive of me as I had been of her. She recommended that I speak with an acquaintance of ours, a Saint Mary's student named Amy whom I had never even realized was a lesbian.

Amy, as it turned out, was co-chair of Gays and Lesbians of Notre Dame/St. Mary's College (GLND/SMC), the same underground group that had placed the tiny newspaper ad the previous year. Their lack of visibility on campus was the result of the fact that they were an unrecognized student organization; they received no funding from the administration of either school and were unable to have speakers or hold meetings or events because only officially recognized student groups were allowed to do so. GLND/SMC's attempts to advertise were severely restricted by the fact that their tiny ads could not make them appear to be a recognized organization; thus, they could not use their name or their acronym, and creative attempts to bypass this rule would be consistently countered by new "amendments" to the advertising regulations. Past applications for recognition had been denied by both schools on the grounds that the group was "philosophically inconsistent with Church teaching." GLND/SMC had been holding discreet meetings on campus since 1986; the organization was supported through dues and donations from its members and friends.

There was another reason for the group's lack of visibility: its members were reluctant to be "out" on campus for fear of being assaulted and harassed. Amy herself had been the victim of rude mail, harassing telephone calls, and vandalism on the part of women in her residence hall. The word "dyke" had been scrawled on her door, her door decorations had been ripped down, and she had answered the phone to hear a loud "Dyke!" shouted before the caller hung up. I apparently had good reason to be afraid of others finding out about me, but my need to break out of my isolation became stronger than my fear.

I began attending GLND/SMC meetings and activities and was happy to find that Miranda, Amy, and I were hardly the only ones. Even though there were only about ten of us at the first meeting, and most of the members were male graduate students from Notre Dame, I felt a strong sense of comfort and safety. At that time, the meetings were focused primarily on political strategies for dealing with the Notre Dame administration, and I learned quite a lot about the group's history and sense of purpose. As the first semester of my senior year progressed, I gradually came to accept the fact that I was a lesbian, that I was *not* abnormal or sinful, that I was capable of living a balanced and fulfilling life just like any other person.

I eventually revealed my sexual orientation to several close friends and to my father. It took some time for them to adjust, but they all ended up being very supportive of me. For the first time in many years, I felt that I was living honestly, that I finally had the freedom to be "real." My friends commented that I seemed much happier and in control of my life.

Unfortunately, while my inner turmoil quieted down, my academic problems did not go away. In December of what should have been my senior year, I was informed that, due to all the classes I had withdrawn from or failed to complete, I had accumulated an insufficient number of credits toward my degree and would now be permanently ineligible for further financial assistance at Saint Mary's College. There was nothing more the counseling center could do to help me, and without financial aid, it would be impossible for me to continue at Saint Mary's. I was offered the option of taking a terminal leave of absence, completing my courses at another school, and transferring those credits back to Saint Mary's. Since this option would still allow me to receive my degree from Saint Mary's, I had the agreement put in writing and took the leave of absence. It would be three years before I entered a classroom again.

Being forced out of school was a major blow for me. I had been an honor student and took pride in my academic ability. I lost much of my intellectual self-confidence and put off returning to school. In the meantime, I chose to remain in Indiana and continue my active involvement with GLND/SMC. The following fall, I was selected to lead GLND/SMC's new coming-out support group.

During the year and a half I led the support group, I realized that there were many students who, like me, faced the coming-out process in fear and confusion because of the indifferent and often hostile environment they found themselves in. When initially contacting me over the telephone, many of them were so terrified of being "outed" to roommates and friends that they refused to give me even their first names. Several of these students were dealing with depression, thoughts of suicide, and academic/motivational difficulties. It became obvious that my own story was by no means a unique one, and that the campus environment was causing too many students to suffer in isolation far too long.

When speaking to these callers, I emphasized that they were not alone, and that meeting other gay, lesbian, and bisexual students was the first step toward overcoming their negative emotions. Most of them had strong feelings about wanting to stay at Notre Dame or Saint Mary's in spite of the homophobic campus climate; as surprising as it may seem, I do not know anyone who transferred to another school. We all felt some sense of pride in our respective schools and knew that we had a right to be there.

It has been five years since the day I first came out to Miranda, and much has changed. Homosexuality has become more visible in society in general over the last few years, and the same has been true of GLND/SMC on campus. Last year, the group's newfound visibility irritated the Notre Dame administration so much that the group was ousted from its meeting place on campus for advertising the meeting location in the student newspaper. The administrations of both schools have historically treated homosexual and bisexual students with indifference at best; at worst, they have been openly hostile. The Notre Dame administration apparently felt that here was an opportunity to sweep "the gay problem" under the rug and render us invisible once and for all.

Their plan backfired. GLND/SMC fought back and alerted local and national media to the campus situation. Within weeks, news of our banishment from campus was everywhere, from the local *South Bend Tribune* to *The New York Times* and even MTV. What is more, we found unexpected support from faculty and even from students of both institutions. Amnesty International and Pax Christi held well-attended demonstrations and rallies on campus in support of GLND/SMC, and the student government distributed buttons with the words "We are all ND/SMC" superimposed over a pink triangle. Nearly every student governing body, as well as the Faculty Senate and the Campus Life Council, not only denounced the administration's treatment of our group but also called upon the university to formally recognize us as an official student organization.

The administration stood firm in its refusal to grant us recognition, but did call for the formation of an ad hoc committee to study gay and lesbian student needs. While the committee was prohibited from considering the possibility that recognition of GLND/SMC might be the best way to meet the needs of those students, the committee members did call for the formation of a "university group" as part of their recommendations. We hoped that the members of GLND/SMC could form the backbone of this group and that it could serve many of the support, educational, and social functions that GLND/SMC had traditionally served.

Unfortunately, the Office of Student Affairs chose to interpret the ad hoc committee's recommendation in the narrowest possible sense. The "university group" was to be severely restricted and so closely monitored that it was doubtful anyone would want to be part of it: it would not be able to hold social gatherings, invite speakers to campus, or plan educational events; there would be no officers or other elected positions; the moderator would be selected by Student Affairs rather than by the members of the group, and this individual would be required to report back regularly to the administration on the group's "progress." We were disappointed, and several ad hoc committee members expressed their frustration as well.

On a more positive note, many of the other recommendations, such as giving workshops in the residence halls on homophobia and what it is like to be gay or lesbian, were supported by the administration. Also, there is no doubt that we have many friends among the faculty and student body, which makes it much safer to be "out" on campus. Homophobia still exists, but it is no longer widely tolerated.

The friendships I made and the education I received at Saint Mary's College have enriched my life tremendously, and will make me proud to be a graduate. But I know that a campus environment more supportive of lesbian and bisexual women could have made a great difference in my college experience. The emotional turmoil and academic setbacks I suffered might not have existed if lesbians had been acknowledged, if a support group had been available, if "out" faculty and staff were present as role models. As an alumna, I intend to work with other concerned members of the college community to make these ideas a reality.

GLND/SMC continues to survive in spite of all the obstacles placed in its path. It was joined in recent years by Gay and Lesbian Alumni/ae of Notre Dame/Saint Mary's College (GALA-ND/SMC), over five hundred members strong and growing every year. Progress has been made, but there is much work yet to be done.

After graduation, Kelly Smith plans on going to optometry school and eventually hopes to help people see more clearly.

the commuter school

In commuter school, the majority of students live off-campus. This creates an unusual social atmosphere and a unique academic environment, since commuter colleges attract more non-traditional (or older) students. In the following essay, Camilla Ragin shows us the daily comings and goings of life at a commuter college.

Keeping the Engine Running

by Camilla Ragin

*e*ight-fifteen a.m. and eighties rock begins my day as an on-campus resident at the University of North Florida, a commuter university. Hoping my roommate will soon turn off her alarm, I roll over to kidnap a few more Z's. My eyes don't open again until 9 a.m. A car horn is beeping and the trash truck is emptying the Dumpster. Coffee drips and shuffling feet provide morning music as I stand by the window. Opening the blinds, I watch the parade of cars. My first thought: no parking competition for moi; my housing sticker gives me license to park wherever I want—ooh, the perks. As the cars creep around the loop, my mind wanders. I leave my room fifteen minutes before I have to be anywhere on campus. I don't fight rush hour or traffic fumes. My commute to class is so much less aggravating. Putting these recurring thoughts on my mental back burner, I concentrate on the parade below. It is after 9 a.m. on a weekday and my university, my home, is full of noise.

Swigging coffee, I complete my morning ritual and hop out the door. People, all shapes, sizes, and colors, bustle along, bags swinging, hands waving, mouths wagging. It's lunchtime and the university is alive. Walking into Human Development, I do a quick visual scan. How does James feel about being in classes with teenagers? James is one of the non-traditional students, a man closer to my parents' age. I take a seat by Marcy, a thirty-something divorcee who came back to school so she could provide a better life for her two kids. How does she balance school, work, and parenthood—and remain so perky? I turn to my left and speak to Jen; she's eighteen and this is her first year away from home (it shows). Every class presents her with a revelation. It's so odd. There are twenty-seven years between James and Jen; there's over ten years between Marcy and me. Sighing, I think of all the stuff the student handbook never mentions, like how some people spend two hours getting to and from school or how bad traffic can cause over half your psych class to be absent, or how a relationship develops when someone is twenty years older than you.

Class is conducted in a circle format because that's more conducive to discussion. Today we're continuing our talk on the childbirth experience. I remember how much I learned last class. It was so weird to speak with an older woman who has given birth twice and an older man who has kids but never went into the delivery room. Then there's Jen, who thought the entire process was gross. James was really open about how men were not expected or invited to share in the birthing experience thirty years ago. I understand the changes in childbirth practices and experiences better because I have the added perspectives of three different generations.

After class, I pass the Green, the "lawn" of the university. The well-tended grass is Crayola-crayon green. Club Fest, showcasing all the on-campus organizations, is taking place today. With 10,708 enrolled, it seems odd more people aren't on the Green, but then again, so many people are on campus only for a few hours. Many commuters are not around long enough to know that Club Fest is happening and are not connected enough for it to matter. But there are a lot of organizations on hand, some fraternities and sororities, a few service groups, the International Student Association, the African-American student union, the conservation club. It's a better turnout than last year's. I just wish every day was like last Saturday, Earth Day Music Fest on the Green, reggae music, local vendors, and plenty of sunshine. It was like a real college event—celebrating a worthwhile cause while meeting new people and feeling globally conscious.

Two classes and I am free for the day; well, I don't have any more classes. Free is relative—meetings with profs, study groups, and homework all require my attention. Quieting the voice in my head, I listen for familiar sounds while I walk. Four-thirty p.m. and the roar is silent. I walk past the bookstore and the metal chairs are empty. Swinging on a metal post, a poster urges me to vote for my student government senators. I see a few faces I recognize, we wave and continue about our business. It's 4:30 and all is quiet. I almost expect to see rolling tumbleweed, there's a certain ghost-town quality this time of day. I think forward to the weekend. I suppose I'll find some people to head out into the city with me. No movie nights in the student rec room, no place to grab a bite to eat (the café is closed on weekend nights). Eating after hours means getting into my car, creeping onto the highway, and driving about five minutes to the nearest restaurant. There's just not enough on-campus life to require all the on-campus services. Out of ten thousand students enrolled, approximately a thousand live on campus.

Eight-fifteen a.m. and eighties rock. It's Friday and my morning ritual is resumed. Out my window I see the the daily parade, and only three or four cars going faster than the posted 35 miles per hour. Ten o'clock arrives and I take the five-minute stroll to the library. I love the library on weekends; there are not a lot of people and I feel like all four floors belong to me. The great part about living on campus at a school full of commuters is being able to access available facilities with little competition—at certain times of the week. The computer lab, the library, the weight room, they are all mine from Friday to Monday. Not many commuters spend their weekends hanging out on campus. Only a few individual voices can be heard; they are soft; the weekend is here.

My tempo is slower and the university reminds me of a Southern stereotype—towering oaks and soft breezes. Walking toward the residence halls, I dodge Rollerbladers and skateboarders. As I look into dorm windows, huge banners and window paint convey messages with meaning only for on-campus residents: "IRHA [Inter-Residence Hall Association] needs you." "Study break Sunday in building W, second floor."

Tossing my bag over my shoulder, I swing open the door

to my dorm room. My roommate, wearing only a T-shirt from Homecoming, sits with jerky fingers at a beeping computer. After two years of rooming, I know when she needs a break—the signs are obvious (scrunched brow and pursed lips). We get along really well. When you live with someone in one room, there are two options: get along or kill each other. Grabbing Cokes and hopping on my bed, we make plans for the next two days. Saturday is for running errands around the city; campus is dead. Saturday night, we're getting together with some friends and going to a movie. I walk to the window. The parking lot is a little emptier. A lot of people leave for the weekend, preferring to go home or visit friends. As the day darkens, a tiny roar gains volume. Friday night echoes with the sounds of residents preparing to go out, to go into the city. Downtown, night clubs, theme restaurants, and the beach all beckon. The roar continues to build, but it cannot compare to the roar of the courtyard at noon.

This is almost the last Friday of the semester and I'll be going home soon. I won't miss the emptying parking lot, the absence of weekend activities, or the events that almost no one attends. I will miss my private weekend library, James's advice, visiting friends at 2:30 a.m. (and not worrying about parents), and the roar that builds, subsides, and eventually becomes silent. Ten thousand people attend my university, but I live only with a thousand.

Camilla Ragin is a psychology major at the University of North Florida and will graduate in 1998.

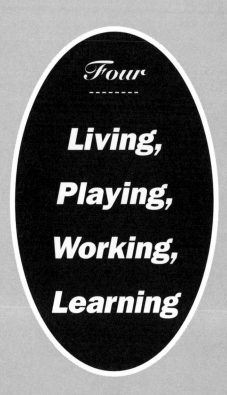

Four

Living,

Playing,

Working,

Learning

living options

In 1972, Oberlin College was featured on the cover of Life magazine as the first college to have coed dorms. Twenty-five years later, practically every residential college in the United States has them. Some have taken it a step further with coed bathrooms, and Antioch College now allows men and women to be roommates. But before we declare single-sex dorms a thing of the past, you should know that many still exist and they do so for a reason.

In the following essays, Anne Sachs gives you the dirt on coed living, and Emily Meier shows you what it's like to have a dorm of one's own.

Girl Music

by Emily Meier

"**W**hat, no boys?" I exclaimed. I couldn't believe it. I had been prompt in picking up my housing lottery number months ago. I had waited in the four-hour "room pick" line, not even leaving my place when I thought for sure my bladder would rupture, only to have a cranky no-nonsense housing woman tell me in an exasperated sigh, "Unfortunately, all the coed dorms are filled." A moment from my senior year in high school flashed before my eyes. I had sworn then I would never live in an all-women's dorm. After all, what fun would that be? "Yeah, coed all the way!" my high school friends chanted in agreement. But now I stood face-to-face with the cranky housing woman. Reality: I would be living exclusively with women. There was no way out of it. I had watched as others argued with the housing woman. Some had vowed to sic their parents on her. But she just shrugged them away and muttered under her breath about "spoiled brat student monsters." I was defeated and in need of the nearest bathroom.

How was I going to tell my roommate and two of my other friends that I, their housing representative, had failed them and we were all doomed to single-sex dorm life? I was cringing as I reported back to them. But, to my surprise, they didn't seem upset at all. Instead, they said things like, "It will be nice to not be always worried about how we look," and "It will be fun, like a twenty-four-hour sleepover." Great, I thought. I had attended many a sleepover in elementary school; all of them inevitably included a nasty fight, tears, and someone being driven home.

It was because of those memories that I began my single-sex dorm experience with a headache. Those first few weeks were an adjustment. Scrunchies, painted picture frames, and clothes were everywhere. For the first time I was in a place where girl stuff ruled. All my life I had been a female in a predominately male household, surrounded by guy stuff. Freshman year of college I lived in a coed dorm and the male presence was still overpowering. But in the all-female dorm, the scene was different. The stench of old running shoes and beer-soaked clothes was replaced by different perfumes and drier-sheet scents. Instead of the thumps of late-night wrestling matches, yelling, and blips and bleeps of Sega games, one could expect to hear giggling, the occasional shriek, and the whirl of hair driers while passing through our dorm.

So what is it like living with all women all the time? I learned that it can be very welcoming. Dorm-room doors are left open during the day, encouraging conversation to drift into the hallway and be added to by anyone interested in the subject at hand. You don't just stay in your room. It's a more communal living atmosphere. Unlike the coed dorm, here singing in the shower and requests shouted by people waiting for a shower are common occurrences. In the all-women's dorm, there is an added element of freedom in the fun, conversations, and dress. Conversations range from the intense, such as the role of the individual in politics and religion, to the casual and personal, such as preferred hair-removal methods. The dress is usually very casual, T-shirt and jeans, and no one hesitates to wander from bedroom to bathroom in just a towel or underwear. On nights when people are going out, especially on the weekends, the hallways become high-fashion runways. Women take turns being models and critics. But, beyond appearances, there is a depth to the all-women's dorm. Your neighbors soon become your support group, cheering section, study group, and family.

My guy friends' reaction to my new living situation was noteworthy. At first, I got comments like, "We're coming to visit you more often." And, "Don't worry, I'll find a place to sleep." I even got the occasional, "What are you doing, living with a bunch of lesbians?" It was interesting to learn just how many stereotypes still exist. I admit, I probably had some of them circling in my mind before I experienced it firsthand.

Now I must discuss the nitty-gritty, for no living arrangement is perfect. There is a phenomenon which I don't believe is recognized by the scientific world, but it is proven time and time again within the walls of women's dorms. I will call this phenomenon, for lack of a better name, simultaneous menstruation. No one knows why it happens, but just ask any woman who has lived with a lot of other women and she will groan with the knowledge of this truth. For some reason, after women have been living together for a few months, their periods coordinate and begin to occur at the same time. This can cause a little bit of tension in your living environment, especially when PMS is shared by all, all at once. It is during these shared couple of weeks that the all-women's dorm resembles the sleepovers of my childhood. During this time, calorie intake is observed by all and the previously unused exercise machines are competitively put to use. Shared PMS creates an environment conducive to petty arguments concerning borrowed items like clothes, CDs, and boyfriends. However, the good news is that tears are easily dried, no one stays mad for long, and not one person I know had to be driven home.

Finally, when the summer came and it was time to leave, I can honestly say I was sad to see everyone go. It was fun to have sisters for a while. As I gathered my clothes from different rooms and returned the items I had borrowed, I secretly thanked the housing woman. I waved goodbye to the women of Curtis West dorm with a mix-tape in hand that a bunch of us had made. I popped it into the car tape deck. And when barely a verse had been played, one of my brothers yanked it out, exclaiming, "Yuck, that's girl music!"

Emily Meier is an English major at Denison University.

The Boys Next Door

by Anne Sachs

*t*he first few weeks of my freshman year, I glued myself to the women in my suite. Hanging out with the people I lived next to seemed an easy way to make friends in a place full of strangers. So I surrounded myself with women, which was something I had never done before. In high school, most of my friends were men. I began to miss the company of men, the fake wrestling used as an excuse to touch the other person, someone to tell you honestly how you looked in a pair of jeans, someone to dance with when you went out to a club. So I peeled myself out of my sweatpants and T-shirt and put on something which reflected effort and a desire to make my breasts known, whipped out the makeup bag, which left a rectangle of dust on my desk when I picked it up, and made myself look presentable to the men on the third floor. The first thing I noticed was the stinging stench of urine embedded in the carpet, both on the men's and on the women's sides. I went to see my friend Brett. He was in the bathroom with a bunch of other guys, making an odd concoction with paints and shaving cream. Then they proceeded to run to the door with the bucket of paint-cream and dump it over the railing, splattering it all over the stairwell. They laughed hysterically, high-fiving each other with their sweaty, paint-stained palms as I walked back down to my floor.

I had forgotten that the people who lived above me were not men. They were boys, boys with animal tendencies. Boys I did not particularly want to see me in a bathrobe, boys I did not particularly want to bother me while I was studying for a midterm. I was beginning to see the benefits of an all-women's floor, the joys of a relatively clean bathroom, of the lack of holes punched in the walls, and those wonderfully endless discussions with other women about being a woman, about feeling fat or lonely or proud of something you said in class.

I realized that women can really listen better than boys. As a freshman, I found it nice to be living in a place where everyone on the floor was willing to admit that she, too, was feeling a little homesick, a little scared, and disconnected from both high school and college. Being sad, homesick, or angry was okay on the all-women's floor in a way which was different from how it was on coed floors. There was a higher level of sensitivity and attentiveness on my floor. I liked the sound of women's voices coming from the hall. It was a sound that felt familiar to me, a sound that made me feel welcome. And to my surprise, I found that there were places to meet people, both men and women, outside of the dorm. But it did take some effort. A date was a very big deal, and it was fairly common during those long winter months in the Adirondacks to hear a fellow floormate wail, "I wanna meet a boy!" Jokingly, a friend of mine once asked, "How do I meet a boy?" She didn't mean for me to answer; what she meant was that it was so easy to have fun with just women friends that for a few months we kind of forgot that something was supposed to be missing from our lives.

I will be a senior at Skidmore this fall, and for the past two years I have chosen to live on a coed floor. And there is something to be said for watching those animals grow up into men. Immediately, you can tell which of the men are upperclassmen; they are the ones who introduce themselves in an effort to get to know you, instead of dumping paint and shaving cream on the carpet in an effort to get some attention. The freedom that college brings is not so over-whelming to them, or to me, anymore and the need to assert that freedom is not so brazen. The intimacy I shared with the men on a coed floor is very different from the relationship I had with those men who lived on the other floors of my freshman dorm. I never try to flirt with the men on my floor; it feels weird to me, like flirting with a cousin or something. I have seen these guys half-naked anyway, and they have seem me in a towel on my way to the shower, so it is some-what desexualized. Plus, dating someone who will live next door to me for the next nine months does not seem like a good idea, in case we broke up.

My mother always said that living with men takes away the mystery, and she is right. But I think the loss of that mystery is positive. I do not want to be mystified by men; I want to understand them, and I want them to understand me. So, yes, they see me with zit cream on my face and no makeup. The men in my hall have seen me sweaty and smelly when I come back from a run, my two breasts squashed into one by a sports bra. They see me at 7:30 in the morning when I have had three hours of sleep and you cannot tell the difference between the color of my pupils and the color of the circles under my eyes. They have seen me cry or laugh uncontrollably, both for no reason at all. And I'm a person to them, not just a woman. Of course, the men are almost inevitably the ones who trash the dorm in a drunken fit. They are usually the ones who are loud when you are trying to study, who leave the TV on, shaking because the volume is so high. They leave week-old pizza in the kitchen. But they listen to me when I ask them to turn down their radios, or to stop bowling in the hallways the evening before my first final exam. I still feel more comfortable asking women to respect my living space, but learning to ask for the same respect from both male and female floormates is important. After graduation, I doubt I will have the option of surrounding myself only with women, and part of my education is proving to be learning how to live with men, even on relatively intimate terms.

Whether I lived on a single-sex floor or a coed one, the level of comfort I felt ultimately reflected the effort I made. Meeting men was harder to do when I was on an all-women's floor, but the rewards of being surrounded by women were worth it for a year. Living with other women felt effortless. After spending a year with mostly women, I found the transition to living with men a challenge, but it got easier with time, and with maturity. Where I live is just not as important to me anymore. I am never in my room, and I have learned to adjust to the constant flux of floormates. I rarely see those women from my freshman year, and it may seem as though it never made a difference what box was checked on the housing questionnaire. But when I think about that first year, about how hard it was, I am grateful for that all-women's floor. I remember sitting in a circle of women in the center of the lounge, making macaroni necklaces for my roommate, who had a bad day and really could use a macaroni necklace. I remember feeling good about being a woman, and I think that was the first time I had ever thought one way or another about it.

Anne Sachs spent the fall semester studying in Bath, England, where the guys are called blokes.

sports

_In 1972, there were about thirty thousand women partici-
pating in collegiate athletics. Today, that number has more
than tripled—with over a hundred thousand playing college
sports. And many of the sports women are competing in
were once exclusively male—like soccer, lacrosse, crew, and
rugby. But this growth in interest, especially interest in
new sports, didn't just happen. All these changes can be
traced back to a law passed in 1972, called Title IX._

_Title IX states that every college and university which
receives federal funds (and most do) must provide equal
opportunities for its male and female students, including
its male and female athletes (more about Title IX on page
208). And while Title IX has created more opportunities for
female athletes, it hasn't cured all the inequities. Every
year, NCAA male athletes receive $179 million dollars more
in scholarships than do female athletes. And while 37 percent of NCAA athletes are women, the average athletic
department devotes only 24 percent of its budget to
women's sports. Today, twenty-five years after its pas-
sage, 90 percent of colleges and universities are not in
total compliance with Title IX._

_Because of this, two congresswomen recently created a
law with you in mind. It's called the Equity in Athletics_

Disclosure Act, and it gives you, the prospective female student-athlete, the power to find out how committed specific colleges are to women's sports (details on page 210). Upon request, colleges are required to make available information on how much money is spent on such things as men's and women's sports programs, men's and women's athletic scholarships, male and female coaches' salaries. In effect, they are required to give you the hard facts on how truly devoted they are to female athletes.

The importance of equal opportunity in athletics is not just about having the chance to play the sport you love. A recent study by the NCAA found that female scholarship athletes had a higher graduation rate than anyone else in college, higher than female non-athletes, and higher than both male athletes and male non-athletes. So, choosing a school which provides you with equal opportunities in sports not only has athletic advantages; it has academic advantages as well.

The following stories are about two athletes in very different situations. Sandra Lind's path led to a winner's circle; Jennifer Boucher's path led to court.

Poor Sports

by Jennifer Boucher

i have always been an athlete. When I was little, I swam, ran, and tree-climbed. Later, I danced and played softball and basketball. In middle and high school I played field hockey, gymnastics, and lacrosse and skied. Sports were so deeply ingrained in my life that I could not imagine life without them. And in high school I didn't have to.

That all changed when I got to college. At the schools I visited, the tour guides always stressed how strong their respective sports programs were. Whenever I asked about lacrosse, my favorite sport, the tour guides for schools without a varsity program were quick to assure me that they had an excellent club or recreational team. Many told me, "You don't need the pressures of varsity anyway." And so, having been assured that, wherever I went, athletics would always be available to me, I resolved to choose a school based solely on its fulfillment of my academic criteria.

Which is how I came to Syracuse. Nationally known for its public-communications school, SU seemed to have everything I needed. Although I was homesick at first, I settled in quickly and was at the club sports office my first day on campus to sign up for the club lacrosse team. I was confident that it would be as fulfilling as any varsity team could be. I waited eagerly for a phone call.

And I waited. And waited.

When the call finally came, weeks later, I copied down all the dates and times of practice and promised to be there. But it was nothing like I had expected.

The club team practiced on a ragged, unlined field a few miles from the main campus. We took buses part of the way there, to the field house, but the last half mile we had to walk. There were no lights, no coach, no locker room, no equipment, nothing. There were no goals, because if we wanted them, we would have to carry them the half mile from the field house. Also, I quickly learned that the club relied mainly on dues from its members to pay referee fees for the few games held each year. Most of the girls there that first day were just out of high school, like me, and were used to a highly organized, competitive program. I could see the disappointment on their faces and knew that even their love of lacrosse wouldn't keep them there. Half of them never came back. Many who stayed were novices—and had never picked up a stick before. Others were out-of-shape juniors and seniors who came to practice once in a while but couldn't run a lap and spent more time socializing than anything else.

Later, I learned how different that first day of practice was for the men's varsity lacrosse team. Walking out on their field, they knew what was coming—some of them, after all, had been heavily recruited out of high school. They had pristine, well-maintained fields, equipment, uniforms, coaches, training facilities, locker rooms, and scholarships.

And so, while the men's team went to that first practice feeling secure and wanted, we huddled on a snowy field feeling shunned and a little bit embarrassed. Maybe women weren't meant to play sports, I thought. Maybe that just wasn't done at Syracuse. Maybe we were making fools out of ourselves for even trying. Sure, the school had some varsity teams for women . . . Maybe the rest of us were just meant to become spectators. But deep down I knew that was wrong.

There is nothing quite like lacrosse, and if you've never played, it's difficult to understand. There is a moment that happens for every player—carrying the ball downfield, you hit this perfect rhythm and everything around you blurs into silence. All you are aware of is the ball in your stick, the crispness of the air, your muscles straining, and the smell of the grass underfoot. Everything is peaceful and perfect and in that one moment the entire world makes sense. After experiencing this, you are never quite the same, and you can never do without it.

The next year I became a captain. And suddenly I understood why the team had to suffer through the conditions it did. This was hard. Since there was no coach and no athletic director to fall back on, my co-captain and I were responsible for everything—scheduling, fields, equipment, paperwork, rosters, everything. If we didn't do something, it would not get done. There would be no season for the club this year if we didn't come through.

What had started as pure enjoyment had become hard work. Lacrosse threatened to take over my social life as well as my academic one. I was always rushing to meet a deadline, to cash a check on time, to make just one more phone call before running to class. I became coach, manager, athletic director, teacher, and referee all in one, when all I wanted to do was play.

But I didn't get to play much that year. It seemed that I was always needed on the sidelines to make substitutions or settle some dispute over calls or scores. Players came to me with personal problems, my co-captain and assistant captain were fighting, and it seemed that I always had a headache. By the end of the year, I was exhausted. But I was not about to give up.

The next year I found a volunteer coach, the father of one of our players, to take over the running of practices. Although I was still responsible for the planning, having a coach meant that I could finally play during practices and at games. It was an uneasy balance of power—since we were a club, we had to be student-run, which meant that ultimately my co-captain and I were still in charge of this coach, who was many years older than both of us.

That year I determined to make my team as good as any varsity team. I began testing the limits. I called the athletic department. I wanted to know why my team couldn't play on the good field, the one with the AstroTurf, the bleachers, and the lights. The one the varsity teams used. I was told that all the club teams could use the field—they had a few hours every Wednesday during which to share it. A dozen club teams at once? That wasn't good enough. I kept pushing, and eventually I got practice time for my team alone on the good field. I also wanted jerseys for my players. After considerable effort, we got those, too. And so I learned to try for what was just a little bit out of reach. I found that people will give in, if only to get you out of their hair and your messages off their answering machines.

That season the club did the best it had in years. We played a full schedule and gave many a varsity team quite a challenge. We actually emerged undefeated from a tournament held in Buffalo that spring—quite an ego-boost. We were talented, we were ambitious, we were proud, and we were good. But we still weren't varsity.

A few of my players had brought the idea of a varsity women's lacrosse team to the athletic department over the past few years. They said their ideas had been considered and then dismissed. But that spring the athletic department announced plans to add some women's teams, lacrosse among them. My team was ecstatic, and I was, too. This new time line meant that I would finally, as a senior, get to try out for a varsity, Division I, women's lacrosse team. I saw this as the fulfillment of all my hard work—finally, I thought, I would get to wear #16, orange and blue, and score a goal for SU.

My elation was short-lived.

Less than a month later, the athletic department said that the previous release had been a mistake, and issued a new time line, pushing lacrosse back yet another year. We were crushed. It was then that I began to question why we weren't varsity. I started to research women's college sports and a law called Title IX that had been passed more than twenty years before. And I found something very interesting: there was no reason why we shouldn't be varsity. The university had been out of compliance with Title IX since the law had been passed.

Title IX is part of the 1972 Educational Amendment Act. It states, among other things, that colleges receiving federal funds must provide equal athletic opportunities and funding for men *and* women athletes proportionate to the number of men and women in the student body. In my research, I found that SU's student body was 51 percent female, but there were at least two male athletes for every female athlete. Although the number of teams for each gender were almost equal, the number of opportunities definitely were not.

We filed a class-action Title IX lawsuit against Syracuse University on May 8, 1995. A lawyer offered to take our case for free. She said she had been waiting years for someone to come to her about Title IX compliance at Syracuse University. And, finally, there we were.

There are eight of us all together, six of my lacrosse players and the captain of the club softball team. I am the unofficial spokesperson, and so I have dealt with much of the publicity, both positive and negative.

We don't know yet what is going to happen. The legal process is long and drawn-out. I have done countless interviews, even done television and radio programs. I have been praised, criticized, and lampooned on radio and in print by people who are convinced we are trying to hurt SU's male athletes by "stealing" their funding. Somehow, I find the energy to keep fighting back. And this fight has truly changed me, changed my entire life. It has made me prioritize what is important.

This issue is no longer about me. It is about all the

others who will come after me. I know now that I will graduate without ever having worn #16 for SU. But I want
other women athletes to have what I never had: the ability
to play their sports without ever having to worry that it all
might be taken away. I want the women athletes of this
school to have the security the men have always enjoyed.
Most of all, I want them never to have to question whether
they are truly athletes.

*As of February 1997, Syracuse University met all of Jennifer
Boucher and her teammate's requests. Under the current plan,
women's lacrosse and women's softball become varsity teams at the
University in the 1997–98 school year. Jennifer graduated last
May and looks forward to playing lacrosse at Syracuse alumnae
games.*

Smells Like Team Spirit

by Sandra Lind

"**S**wimmers, clear the water." I pulled my goggles
over my eyes and knelt down by the starting block. I splashed
some water on my body, wiped my face, and stood behind
my lane. I was a little cold from the Hawaiian breeze that
night, but I was too focused to care. The whole training
camp was turning out to be filled with breakthroughs for
me, both in workouts and in meets. Before I left for camp,
my boyfriend of two and a half years and I decided to break
up. Despite this change in my life, maybe because of it, I felt
a sense of freedom. I realized that I wouldn't be lost without

him and his support. I think I found some strength that was there all along.

"Swimmers, step up." With *Colorado State* imprinted on my cap and suit, I stepped up on the block. As co-captain, I have always felt more support from my teammates than pressure to be a leader and scorer. Hearing my name called from various directions, knowing my friends and teammates were cheering for me, I was psyched up and ready to swim fast.

The whistle sounded. I bent over and shook my hands.

"A hundred-yard breaststroke. Take your mark . . ." I stepped up to the edge and grabbed the sides of the block.

At the sound of the starting whistle, I propelled myself into the noise of the air and dove into the silence of the water. I felt so good; nothing could stop me. After a four-laps sprint, I touched the wall and looked up at my time. It was my fastest ever and the fastest in our conference that season. I saw the reaction of my coaches and teammates and felt happy to be a contributing part of the team's success. I felt I had found something in me that was strong, something I was good at, that gave me a sense of significance.

Keeping the windows open at night let us wake up not only to the sun and smell of Hawaii but also to the sound of a beeping garbage truck. "Goddamnit!" Tracy usually censored that phrase for me, but at 6:45 in the morning she had neither the energy nor the inclination to watch what she was saying. We had to get up in fifteen minutes anyway.

No one ever said anything until we were a little more awake. Marni turned on the coffeemaker. Lori was in the bathroom. Tracy was still in bed. And I got my stuff together for practice.

"Do you think we'll need our running shoes?"

The alarm went off. "Goddamnit!" Turning it off, I laughed at Tracy's little battle with morning noises.

"Yeah, I think we're going to do weights and stairs after practice."

After coffee, and the usual run around the hotel room searching for my swimsuit, we were finally ready to go downstairs to the vans.

"Maybe we'll end practice early since we have a meet tomorrow" was the last thing I heard before I dove into the water. By the end of practice, I wanted to laugh at the irony of the statement. Christmas training camp was always fun, but easy it definitely was not. With my mind and body exhausted, I could only smile. I had a good practice and swam fast times despite my tired body and breaking will. If there was ever a point in practice when I didn't think I could move my arms, much less swim anything hard, there was a always a coach yelling, "Come on, Sand," or a teammate saying, "Good job. Let's go!"

Training camp had some bad points, though. I had only ten days to spend with my family, compared to the four weeks my roommates at school got with theirs. We also had to pay for our own ticket and some of our food, unlike the situation on our other travel trips. And of course, the training was fiercely intense. But as I floated there after practice, looking up at the sun-drenched sky, I felt such freedom. I didn't have to worry about going home after practice, studying for a test worth a third of my grade, or getting enough sleep to make it to workout at six the next morning. Also, there weren't any tests or classes to make up. Most of my professors are nice, but there are a few that aren't as accommodating. Before our Nebraska trip, one of my professors sneered when I explained to him that my absence is excused by the school. Still floating, I stared up and thought how much I loved being in this exact place.

After training camp in Hawaii, we came back to our Colorado college town to finish the last stretch of our competitive season and to begin the spring semester. Throughout the season and in previous ones, I had some downs as well as ups. Struggling with some minor injuries in competition, I learned some humbling lessons. Now, with a couple of months to the Western Athletic Conference Championships, I needed to put my struggles behind me and focus on our goal to take the conference championship title. However, that wasn't my only focus.

Down at the mailbox, I tore open the manila envelope. I couldn't believe it! I was chosen to be interviewed by the physical-therapy department at the graduate school I most wanted to attend. I read the rest of the information in my apartment. They wanted another essay, and an interview was scheduled for a couple of days before we left for conference. Trying to make decent grades in biochemistry and similar classes was already a challenge; now I had to prepare for one of the most important interviews of my life. The athletic department helped by arranging for the athletes to register for class before the rest of the student body, to minimize conflicts between class and practice times. They also provided tutors for us. However, I got the most support from the people around campus. People would talk to me about the sport, commending the teams' success and work ethic. It made the conference title goal a bigger thing. It was no longer for the twenty girls I trained with; it was for the school. The busy months passed quickly. Before I knew it, conference had arrived and we were in San Antonio vying for the championship.

It was definitely one of the most intense moments I've experienced. I looked around the circle of these women who had become my family. I spent a good part of each day with these swimmers and have seen their struggles and fears. I have experienced their joys and accomplishments. I wondered where again I'd find an opportunity to expand, push, better, and test myself, and be able to share that with those around me doing the same. I looked down and waited for the results, gripping the hands on either side of me.

They announced the Coach of the Year and the Swimmer of the Year. Both were from our team. We got even more anxious, some of us crying, all of us gripping harder the hands we held. It was hitting me that our goal of conference champions was looking like a reality. I admit I was crying like a baby. I had waited four years for this. We had finished second the previous few years. Four years of "this year we'll do it." Four years of putting what seemed like everything we had into a goal.

"In second place is BYU." We all went nuts. Through the screams I heard, "And the 1995–96 WAC champions, the women of Colorado State." It was real. We did it. The camera flashed, capturing the moment. All of us crowded on the winner's platform, holding the trophy with our hands raised above our heads in victory.

I embraced this afternoon by doing absolutely nothing. The only commitment I had for the rest of the day was dinner at the university president's house. He had invited the team over to celebrate our victory. The rest of the spring semester was one of the most unique times of my life.

I got my acceptance letter to physical-therapy school the day after I got back from the conference. I now had a direction after graduation. And there was no spring training, no early mornings, no practices inside a building on a beautiful day. But I missed it and I knew that an incredible time in my life had come to a close. I was given this awesome opportunity not only to go to college but also to be a student-athlete. I walked onto the team with no athletic scholarship and worked my way to be a Division I NCAA scholarship-athlete. I developed my body, mind, and spirit by continuously challenging myself to find strength that I did not know was there. I learned what it meant to succeed, to fail, to give, to receive, to lead, to follow, to begin something, and eventually, how to let it go. And all this I learned in that school, in that pool.

Sandra Lind is in physical-therapy school, learning how to make other people strong.

work-study

Over the past fifteen years, the average cost of attending private college has increased by 90 percent, and the average cost for public colleges has increased 100 percent. At the same time, median family income has risen just 5 percent. And although women in college receive a higher proportion of the financial aid awarded (which makes sense, since women are 55 percent of college students), the average female student's financial-aid award is smaller than the average male's. The good news is that there is more financial aid out there than ever before (in 1995, there was almost $47 billion dollars available, 70 percent more than ten years ago), and there are also sources of financial aid just for women (see page 219).

Some colleges may offer you work-study in your financial-aid package. In the following essay, JoEllen Perry shows you the ins and outs of being a full-time student with a part-time job.

Work It, Girl

by JoEllen Perry

I waitressed most weekends during high school, so by the time I received a work-study job as part of my financial-aid package for college, combining work with study was a normal part of life, and a steady source of income. At Kenyon, the salary you receive for a work-study doesn't get incorporated into your tuition payments. It comes to you as a cold hard check all your own. I've been glad for these jobs both because it's comforting to know that money (even if it isn't much) will be reliably coming in and because they engender a feeling of responsibility and capability, completely different from the satisfaction of finishing a good paper or acing a test. Work-study keeps a variety of skills active: it helps you maintain your perspective, helps prevent you from losing yourself in the pressured arena of academic standards. And that's good, because college will be over in four years and you'll probably forget pretty quickly the specifics of most of the papers you write, but you'll always need a job—and the ability to work hard at and keep a job which you may or may not like will help you long after college is over.

I talked to some friends with work-study experiences and also drew upon my own; here are some of the jobs we've had and what they've been like:

Across the board, we agreed that our least favorite jobs

had been those assigned to us as first-year students. After we'd been at school for a while and knew generally what was available on campus, we could go after the jobs which most attracted us. Before we came to school, though, we were asked to fill out a sheet detailing our specific talents, capabilities, and previous job experience, so the Kenyon staff could try (so they said) to match us up with the jobs which best suited us. I don't know where they got the idea that I'd have a knack for getting up at 7:30 a.m. two days a week to reshelve books that students had left lying around the library the night before, or that I was the perfect person to type tiny labels on art-history slides, but they did. And although they were wrong, I was lucky to have *two* jobs; Kenyon usually restricts students to one. The library couldn't offer me enough hours to equal the pay that I'd been promised in my financial-aid package, so Kenyon provided a supplementary job. Kenyon's generosity goes the other way, too—many of the people I talked to stressed the fact that here work-study truly puts a priority on studying: if you're having a rough academic week, most supervisors understand and will let you cut out early, or cut out completely, so you can concentrate on your schoolwork. A major asset of work-study is that it compels you to manage your time, to learn how to balance your various responsibilities.

Many incoming students are assigned work in the dining halls. This is reputedly the worst job on campus (the dish rooms have been compared to the ninth circle of Dante's Inferno), but most who've actually done this work say it's not so bad. One student, now a junior, who has had the job since his first year, says that it has become one of his favorite things about Kenyon. These jobs are somewhat atypical: you work primarily with non-students, with a local and full-time cafeteria staff (as opposed to an intramural referee or a box-office attendant, who would work mostly with students). In such a small collegiate community, contact with people outside the academic world is rare. My friends with dining-hall duty were grateful for the regular dose of "reality" their work-studies provided. Although work-study keeps you aware of the monetary cost and personal value of your education, it's still easy to forget that a world other than the campus exists, that the "real world" lives at a different pace and has different priorities and expectations than do college students.

Scott said that working in the dining hall inspires him to work hard academically—that the value of his education has increased because he's seen the opportunities school will provide him with, in comparison to what his co-workers have not had. His work-study makes him aware, too, of all that's *given* to us at school, all the services we take for granted, because he has to work physically to make the food service come together.

Erica mentioned that for the first few weeks relations between students and full-time workers were tense. She and her student co-workers were automatically and silently given the worst duties. One day, Erica and her supervisor somehow got to talking, and Erica asked the woman outright whether she believed that all Kenyon students were rich. The woman said yes. "Well, I'm not," Erica replied, "and that's why I have this job." The woman immediately changed her attitude, enough for the two of them actually to become friends. This tension can also exist with other students. My friends and I with work-studies, especially the first year, did feel somewhat set apart from and resentful of our peers who didn't have to work. But as you get used to your job, learn how to incorporate it into your life, and come to appreciate it for what it *adds* to your academic mind-set and social circle, this feeling becomes less and less of an issue.

From sophomore to senior year, I had a string of jobs, and usually more than one at a time. Although the rules concerning multiple jobs exist for a good reason (to ensure that all students who've been promised a job get one, that no one's shortchanged while someone else rakes in all the hours and money, and that no one sacrifices his or her grades for a paycheck), very often students who've been promised a job don't take it, or lose it somehow, and so there are extra slots to fill. There are also lots of jobs which aren't official work-studies (that is, they aren't sponsored by the financial-aid office but instead are given out by a department of the college for that department's specific and possibly temporary needs). Finding and securing these kinds of jobs can be tricky and might take more luck or pluck than talent or financial need. I was in a tough English class with a blind woman, remembered that she'd advertised in the school paper for people to read assignments to her, and offered to be her reader. Not only did I get a semester job and a chance to review and discuss the difficult material with her, but we became friends and I became aware of a whole new way of learning, and of how much I took for granted as a student with sight.

I got another unofficial job by following up on an advertisement for a shuttle-bus driver. Kenyon, a school of two thousand students, exists in a village of five hundred people—the closest grocery store, Taco Bell, or bowling alley is about ten miles away, and many students don't have cars, so every day a shuttle takes students into town for free. There are also weekly shuttles to and from the nearest major city (Columbus, Ohio), and special trips to pick up college bigwigs, such as trustees or guest lecturers, from the airport. At best a mediocre driver, I probably upset some hung-over stomachs driving that huge boat of a bus on Saturday mornings. But it was fun, a rare opportunity to drive (on this tiny and very walkable campus), and an easy way to meet people.

There are official work-studies which are all study and no work, and for which you can get snazzy, résumé-beefing titles. These jobs are pretty sought-after and usually go to upperclassmen. For two years, I was an Audio-Visual Equipment Operator. Technically, I should know how to set up the reels of a 16-millimeter film projector (those ancient clicking machines from middle school), or find the volume knob on a many-buttoned laser-disc system. But, aside from setting up an occasional slide show to accompany a lecture, all I really did was wait for someone to come in and check out a piece of equipment. Since hardly anyone ever did, I got paid for doing homework.

All work-study jobs pay a flat minimum wage. But if you want to make more than the average Joan, all you need do is take off all your clothes and sit naked, and very still, in front of an art class for a couple of hours a week. Nude models make about 25 percent more an hour than any other person on work-study on campus. I never got up the gumption to do it, but there are plenty of people who don't mind sitting next to someone in Shakespeare class who, figuratively, has caught them with their pants down.

School jobs put you in positions of prominence: people see you working and might ask you for help when you're off-duty. Friends who work in the college writing center, a place where students can come to other students to get grammar and proofreading help with their papers before they're officially due, say that they're often approached after hours—at meals, for instance—with a request to look over someone's work. There are other student staff jobs which require, and draw upon, a higher level of commitment than regular work-study. Some foreign-language buffs become assistant teachers, teaching daily supplementary classes to intro-level language students.

While I was deciding where to go to college, I rambled the campus of a certain Ivy League school which shall remain nameless, with a tour guide who walked backwards as if it was her job. That is, she didn't face forward *once*, not even during long silences between tour stops or to cross the street. She unnerved me, and honestly was part of the reason I chose not to apply to that school. Guiding tours may be the closest thing to a high-pressure job that work-study can offer; truly, a tour guide can make or break a prospective student's impression of the school. There are also work-study power trips, jobs which elevate one above the masses, such as student-interviewer positions. These typically go to seniors who've made it through a grueling selection process, for the privilege of perusing top-secret application files and hanging out with prospective students for about a half hour, and then offering their educated opinion to the admissions committee about whether or not this person has the potential to succeed and to be happy at Kenyon.

In my senior year, I'm a house manager, something like a CEO, of an upperclassmen dorm. This is neither an official work-study nor an unofficial job. House managers and resident advisers are student staff members of the college. RAs are basically better paid HMs, who work in first-year halls. They put significantly more time and effort into their new recruits than HMs need to invest in students who already know the ropes. The application process for these jobs, which are full-time responsibilities, includes intense interviewing and training. The training workshops were jam-packed with all kinds of imaginary tragedies from which we were supposed to learn how to handle the real thing, and while they were fun and informative, I didn't really take them seriously until I faced a similar scenario. During the first week of school, someone slipped a note under my door, saying that she was having trouble adjusting to school and could she come talk to me about it. My heart pounded for a while, and even as I sat with this woman, held her hand, listened to and I hope helped her, I kept thinking, "Wow, it's really happening!"

The house-manager job isn't always so heartwarming. I've had to mop vomit off stairs and clean up a filthy lounge after a party. But, like any job, and probably like any endeavor, you get out of it what you put into it. Although it sounds like a cliché, I think work-study enables you to learn a ton about yourself and about other people in ways which a strictly academic experience cannot provide. Scott, the guy who stuck it out in the cafeteria, believes that his work-study has changed his perspective on life, and he believes that the college should make the jobs mandatory for all students. I wouldn't go as far as requiring that everyone do a work-study, the way you take a class, but I do think my work-study experiences have been as invaluable, educational, and worthwhile as any class I've taken.

Last year, JoEllen Perry graduated Phi Beta Kappa and summa cum laude.

21

women's studies

Here's a test. Count all the women you studied in high school. Take as long as you like...

That was probably the shortest exam you've ever taken. And it's no fault of your own. Most high schools don't teach about women, which is unforgivable. Women have had profound effects on society. This is something you'll find out if you choose a college with a women's-studies department.

What you'll also find is that the presence of a women's-studies department will affect your education no matter what major you choose. If you plan on becoming a politician or a lawyer, you need to know about the gender gap and how our legal system has treated and is treating women. If you plan on being an economist, you need to know how pay inequity and the growing number of women in the workforce affects the economy of our country. If you want to be a sociologist, you need to know how access to birth control and freedom of choice has changed our society. As a psychologist or educator, you need to know how girls are socialized differently from boys and why many girls suffer a self-esteem crisis in their teens. Because women's studies is interdisciplinary, its courses range from history, psychology, literature, and the arts, to religion, business, science, media, and education within a female context.

Without an official women's-studies department, it is rare to have the opportunity to learn about these issues.

And most important, if a college doesn't believe women's ideas, accomplishments, and lives are worthy of being studied and understood in the same way men's lives are, it should make you wonder whether its female students' ideas, accomplishments, and lives are appreciated in the same way as those of its male students. It should also make you wonder whether it will be a place where you will receive a complete education.

In the following essay, Shannon Coleman shows you why women's studies made her question everything she ever learned.

Taking Credit

by Shannon Coleman

Notes slip between fingers and under desks. Muffled giggles and whispers come from the back of the room. Brian, two rows to my left, silently mimics Mr. Brown, who, oblivious, stands at the lectern talking about the French Revolution. In this history class, as with most of the courses in my high school, we concentrate upon the "important material," significant dates, wars, major political and social movements. Events and ways of thinking that center on (or at least are studied from the vantage point of what most textbooks and teachers seem to center on)—men. Today's lecture is no exception.

This fact suddenly strikes me, and mustering my courage,

I raise a hand and wait until this "old school" teacher acknowledges my presence. "What about women?" I finally inquire. "Did they have a role in the revolution?" Mr. Brown pauses a moment and bursts into laughter. "We can't waste our time upon such nonsense," he comments. "Studying the history of women is comparable to studying the history of dogs. It's simply nonexistent."

Few teachers were as blatantly outspoken as Mr. Brown, but this was the message I received all through high school. And not only in history class. In other social science, humanities, fine arts, and math and science courses, women, if mentioned at all, were discussed in passing, as an appendage. The female gender, the curriculum implicitly directed, had contributed little worthy of reference.

September 1993. My hand shakes uncontrollably as I enter Friendship Village. Perhaps the distinct nursing-home odor triggers my fear. The musty mixture of medicine and urine reminds me of visiting Great-grandma Harriet at Tender Care Center. I still remember wandering the yellow corridor as a little girl, pigtails bouncing, eyes half shut, hiding behind Mom's skirt. People with sagging skin waited aimlessly in the hallway, muttering to themselves, or to one another, or, occasionally, to me. It was funny how, after a few minutes, the stench faded. Everything blended in, the wheelchairs, the fake plants in the lobby, even Great-grandma.

"This will be different," I assure myself. A first-year college student, I am fourteen years older now and without a hiding place. And, even more important, I have come on a mission. My friend Melanie and I plan to interview Margaret, one of the residents, for our seminar entitled Writing

Women's Lives. Our assignment is to gather background information through a series of interviews and, eventually, to write her biography.

Margaret, hooked to an IV, sits propped up in a hospital bed. Her friendly smile immediately puts me at ease. The spunky eighty-six-year-old proceeds to chronicle her life. She was born in 1907. Her parents spent the first years of her life serving as missionaries in China. Education became a major priority for Margaret upon her arrival in the States. Unlike many women of her generation, she went to college, actually worked her way through, and decided to have a career as a teacher instead of being a wife.

I anxiously await our next scheduled visit with Margaret. Melanie and I are lucky. Several of our classmates are having a difficult time with their interviews. Some of the ladies are forgetful; others are unwilling to open up. This certainly isn't a problem with Margaret. Her stories offer both entertainment and insight.

"I must seem ancient to you," Margaret says at our last session. But she doesn't. Despite her white hair and wrinkles, despite the fact that she was nearly seventy years old when I was born, she doesn't. At the end of the interview, Melanie and I present Margaret with a card, thanking her for the help. Tears stream down her face as she reads our colorful construction. "Thank *you* for listening to me," she says.

On the bumpy car ride home, I close my eyes and reflect upon the experience. This project has certainly changed my thinking about the past. It makes me wonder how many women's stories, like Margaret's, have been ignored or forgotten.

March 1995. "What do you learn in women's-studies courses, anyway? How to knit and gossip?" teases Brady. We are sprawled out in the dormitory lounge, with piles of books and papers everywhere, trying to study for midterms. I give my obnoxious friend one of my infamous looks, ignore his ignorant words, and continue with my reading. But Brady's constant gibes get on my nerves. Indeed, the women's-studies courses that I've taken in college have been among the most challenging and engaging classes, intellectually and otherwise, that I've ever had. Through candid class discussions and meaningful projects such as Margaret's biography, I've learned how to take women's lives, my own included, more seriously.

Some of this knowledge was gained indirectly, through classroom dynamics. Most of the courses I've taken have been predominately, if not exclusively, comprised of women. Studies have shown that teachers call on men more frequently in discussions. Women, moreover, are often hesitant to answer questions and contribute, even if they have meaningful insights. Dr. Anderson used to point such information out to our women and religion class. "Look at yourselves!" she would direct to the circle of desks. "Women are taught to be polite, to take up as little space as possible." And, sure enough, when I looked around, I noticed that all the women were courteously situated, with their ankles crossed. The two men sprawled out comfortably with their legs wide open. "Know that it's O.K.—and important even—to take up space and use those voices," Anderson told us.

Certainly, the very *context* of women's-studies courses demonstrates the significant value of female lives. By focusing on how women affect interdisciplinary fields ranging from economics to psychology to political science, this curriculum explores how half the human race has historically and currently shaped and influenced the world in important, meaningful ways. In a society where women vote, purchase the majority of consumer goods, and are entering the work-force in numbers greater than ever before, this is certainly not information for people like my friend Brady to scoff at or ignore. Not if they want to survive in the modern world.

In retrospect, I feel both enraged by and sorry for my old high school teacher and his sexist, outmoded thought. Two years after I took Mr. Brown's class, my women's-history professor noted that women served as firebrands, igniting the French Revolution. According to historian Genevieve Fraisse, during the uprisings of 1795, as in 1789 and May 1793, women sounded the tocsin, beat drums in the city streets, mocked the authorities and the military, enlisted re-luctant bystanders, and invaded stores and workshops. Only later did men join their mothers, wives, and daughters in demonstrations. If Mr. Brown thinks that such information is "nonsense," he had better update and check his sources. And he best watch carefully as younger generations of strong-willed, educated women mark our changing society. Throughout history, women have changed the world, and we always will. It's time we take credit for it.

Shannon Coleman is a senior at Kalamazoo College and plans to go to Divinity School to become a minister and shake up the institutionalized church.

Five

In

the

Know

a note on standardized tests: is the SAT your friend?

The main function of the SAT is to predict how well, academically, a student will do in the first year of college. The score on this test is supposed to help an admissions department determine whether a student can meet the academic requirements established by the college. So, from an admissions standpoint, if one applicant scores lower on the SAT than another, it is assumed that the lower-scoring student will earn a lower grade point average in college than the person with the higher SAT score. All this would be fine and good if the SAT actually did what it is supposed to do, but it does not. Women score on average 39 points lower than men on the SAT, but they consistently achieve higher grades in college than do their male counterparts. In all majors other than chemistry, women with lower SAT scores than men earned grade point averages equal to those of the men. Women with scores identical to those of men earned higher grade point averages than men across all majors. And even though these tests have been found not to serve their purpose in predicting how well the majority of college-bound students (females) will do in college, many colleges continue to use the SAT as a primary admissions tool, lowering the chances that a female will be accepted to the school of her choice rather than a similarly qualified male. A study in the use of the SAT in undergraduate admissions at the University of California at Berkeley found that the number of women admitted into each class is reduced by about 5 percent, or 200 to 300 females, because of the SAT.

The use of this standardized test not only hurts women in admissions; it also hurts women financially. Qualification for the National Merit semifinalist status is based solely on PSAT scores (a test used to predict SAT scores), which have also been found to underestimate a female student's potential. Each year, approximately 60 percent of National Merit Scholarships are awarded to boys, even though 55 percent of the applicants are female. The test's bias deprives many equally qualified girls from receiving full-ride scholarships to college, scholarships provided by corporations and the National Merit Scholarship Corporation, as well as immeasurable prestige.

What should you do, then? First, you should know that there are many colleges, approximately 250, which don't require applicants to submit standardized-test scores. Because the test is shown to be gender-biased, many colleges no longer use it when judging an applicant's qualifications. These colleges are called SAT and ACT optional colleges, and since they have eliminated the standardized-test requirement, most have found they've gained diversity in their student body and there has been no reduction in quality as measured by grade point average, retention rate, and graduation rate. Many of these schools have also found the test-score option to be more popular with female applicants. At Dickinson College, 11 percent of male and 17 percent of female applicants took the optional route. At Lafayette, twice as many women as men chose not to submit: 20 percent, as compared to 10 percent. These SAT and ACT optional colleges include some of the very elite universities, small private liberal-arts colleges, public colleges, and historically black colleges. You can obtain an up-to-date list of SAT and ACT optional colleges by sending a self-addressed, stamped envelope to FairTest (see page 221 for more information).

Second, you should know that the gender scoring gap is significantly reduced for students taking the ACT. The SAT and the ACT are scored on different scales. The SAT scale is 400–1,600 and the ACT scale is 4–36. For 1996 college-bound seniors, the SAT gender gap was 4 points on verbal and 35 points on math, for a total of 39 points. The ACT gender gap was 0.2 points, which is the equivalent of 8 or 9 points on the SAT. While there is still some disparity, it is lessened to a remarkable degree for students taking the ACT. Most schools which accept SAT scores also accept ACT scores. And while there is no scholarship-based program like the National Merit Scholarship associated with it, the ACT may better represent your potential to an admissions office than will the SAT. Your guidance counselor should have information on when and where the ACT is given in your area. You can request registration material which includes dates and locations of the test, and receive a free booklet called "Preparing for the ACT," by contacting the ACT office at (319) 337-1270.

Most important, you should figure out which test best suits your test-taking skills. Your high school guidance department and local library should have books which include samples of both tests. Try a practice test of each and see which you feel more comfortable taking and score better on. There are computer software programs that range in price from about $35 to $60 which can help guide you through the test-taking process. There are also sites on the Internet which offer practice tests and analyses of your test results, including information on which sections you are strong on and which sections you need to work at (see page 221 for more information). Preparatory courses for the SAT and ACT are very expensive, but they have been found to raise students' scores. You may find, since the ACT is more commonly taken by students in the Midwest, that the big test-preparatory companies, like the Princeton Review or Kaplan, are more likely to offer SAT classes at their West and East Coast sites. Both companies also publish ACT and SAT practice books with tips and strategies to improve your score. You may learn just as much from a book as you would from a course, and save hundreds of dollars.

the questionnaire: important things to find out about the colleges of your choice

This section has questions you may want to ask of colleges. Often, the answers to these questions are provided by departments other than admissions. There are suggestions before each part as to where you can obtain specific information, as well as reasons why these questions are important. You may want the answers to some questions but do not feel comfortable calling and asking them yourself. If so, have a parent call or have a guidance counselor request the information from the department.

The President

You wouldn't move to a new country without knowing the politics of the president in power. This logic should also be used when looking into colleges. The president sets the agenda for a school. The president selects the people who will decide what you will learn, who will teach it to you, what events take place on campus, the rules by which students must abide, and how the college will change in the future. You will be spending four years of your life, and a lot of money, at the college he or she leads. You have every right to know what the president has done, is, or will be doing. Contact the president's office or the public affairs of-

fice, and/or check out issues of the campus newspaper on-
line to get this information:

How long has s/he been president?_____

What are some of the important things s/he has done?_____

_____

_____

What has s/he done before becoming president?_____

_____

_____

If s/he is new, does s/he have bold changes in mind? What
are they?_____

_____

_____

The Faculty

The professors a college hires indicate whose ideas and perspectives are valued most. The ratio of women to men who
get tenure (the coveted rank which allows professors freedom in regard to what they teach and the security of knowing their jobs are permanent) will give you some insight into
how much a college respects the ideas and scholarship of
women. This information can usually be found through the
office of the Dean of Faculty, Institutional Research, or the
Office of Admissions.

What is the ratio of female to male faculty?_____

What is the ratio of female to male tenured faculty?_____

What percentage of the faculty are people of color?_____

If you have a field of interest, look into the faculty in that department:

What are their accomplishments, their published books, etc.?

_____

_____

Is there a political trend in the department; i.e., conversative vs. liberal?_____

Women's Studies

At most colleges, women's studies is interdisciplinary, which means it relates to many different fields of study, such as history, literature, psychology, sociology, economics, and politics. Since most schools don't intergrate women's studies throughout the curriculum, it's up to the women's-studies departments to teach us the important role and influence women have had in societies throughout history. The presence of a women's-studies department can affect your education dramatically, no matter what major you choose. The admissions department and/or the academic dean's office can provide you with answers to the following:

Does the college offer women's studies as a major or minor? If not, why not?_____

_____

_____

Do they integrate women's history and scholarship throughout the curriculum?_____

_____

_____

Health Facilities

The services provided by health centers differ from college to college. Some are opposed to providing birth control to students (which can become a serious problem if you are sexually active and do not have a convenient way of getting off campus to buy some). Some offer gynecological care; others do not. The availability and quality of these services will be very important to you when you're at school, so it's a good idea to look into them now. For answers to the following questions, contact the health centers or clinics at each of the colleges you are considering.

Does the school provide and accept student health-insurance plans?_____

Does the clinic provide gynecological care?_____

Does it provide birth control? What kinds?_____

_____

Campus Crime

The Student Right-to-Know and Campus Security Act of 1990 (more about this law on page 211) requires colleges to keep a record of crimes committed on campus and to make this information available to prospective students and parents upon request. Some colleges have avoided reporting the most serious offenses, like rape and sexual assault, by using campus courts systems that seek penalties other than criminal prosecution, which would require the college to report such crimes. You should request the security report from a college security department and then follow up with the women's center and the on-line student newspaper to get a more comprehensive picture. Also, the college is required to report only crimes against students that were committed on campus. A study by Safe Campuses Now at the University of Georgia, Athens, found that 107 of the 305 crimes committed against students occurred off campus. In college, you will spend a lot of time off campus and you may decide to live off campus at some point. Calling a local police department to find out about crimes committed against people age 18–24, and reading the local newspaper, can give you some idea of how safe the surrounding area is for students. The following questions can be posed to the college's security office, which is also where you can request a crime report:

What crimes, and how many, were committed on campus in the past several years?_____

_____

_____

How many students were victims of crime off campus? What crimes?_____

_____

_____

Were there any rapes or sexual assaults on campus recently? How were they handled?_____

_____

_____

What procedures are used to insure that students are safe on campus?_____

_____

_____

Does the campus have a written policy against sexual harassment by faculty and staff?_____

What about a written policy against student-to-student sexual harassment?_____

Athletics

In 1996, the Equity in Athletics Disclosure Act went into effect. It requires any college which receives federal funds (almost all do) to make available to prospective students, parents, and any interested person a detailed report on the college's men's and women's sports programs. The report must include a gender breakdown of scholarships, number of varsity teams, budget for teams, and salaries of coaches. It is meant to be a tool for prospective female students who are interested in playing collegiate sports and want to see how committed a certain school is to its female student-athletes. Since this is a new law, some athletic departments are not as familiar with the requirement as they should be. Remember, by law they must make this available to you. If you are hoping for an athletic scholarship and do not feel comfortable calling an athletic department for this information, ask your high school guidance counselor or high school coach to request it. The following questions will be answered in the Equity in Athletics Disclosure Act report, which can be requested through each college's athletic director's office:

Are there as many varsity teams for women as there are for men?_____

Are there an equal number of male and female varsity athletes?_____

Do women get as much athletic scholarship money as do men?_____

Social Aspects

A women's center, a gay, lesbian, and bisexual students' union, a black students' association are all important groups that serve the interests of many students. The presence and official acknowledgment of these groups indicate a commitment on the part of the administration to diversity and to fulfilling the needs of many students. The following questions can be answered by the student affairs office:

Is there a women's center on campus?_____

What kind of services does it provide?_____

Is there a gay, lesbian, bisexual student group on campus?

_____

Is it supported by the administration?_____

Is there a black student's organization on campus?

_____

Are there any other cultural organizations on campus?

_____

If the school has a Greek system, what percentage of the student body are members?_____

your rights:
laws for college-bound girls
and college women

The following laws were created with you in mind.

Title IX

Title IX is the part of the Education Amendments of 1972 that prohibits sex discrimination in educational institutions that receive any federal funds. It states:

No person in the United States shall, on the basis of sex, be excluded from participation in, be denied the benefits of, or be subjected to discrimination under any educational program or activity receiving Federal financial assistance.

Title IX applies to all educational programs in an institution that receives any federal funds. The majority of schools in this country, from elementary schools through colleges, receive federal funds, including private colleges, which receive federal funds through financial-aid programs such as Pell grants.

Title IX guarantees equal opportunity in all aspects of education. Today, most Title IX cases brought against high schools, colleges, and universities concern equal athletic opportunities for women and men. Title IX covers three major areas of high school and college athletics: athletic financial assistance; effective accommodation of student interests and abilities; and other program components.

If educational institutions are found to be in violation of Title IX, their federal funding can be taken away. However, in all Title IX compliance cases so far, institutions found in violation have agreed to comply with the law rather than lose funding.

In February 1992, the Supreme Court provided a new tool for enforcement of Title IX by ruling that plaintiffs can seek monetary damages in Title IX cases. Before that ruling, the only solution that courts offered was that the school must stop the discrimination. Now that courts are allowed to award monetary damages, schools that are found guilty of sex discrimination can suffer a much harsher penalty. As a result, many schools now take Title IX much more seriously than in the past.

The Office for Civil Rights (OCR) of the Department of Education is the government office that enforces Title IX. Complaints about possible Title IX violations may be filed with this office.

Resources with detailed information about Title IX:

Breaking Down the Barriers: A Legal Guide to Title IX, by Ellen J. Vargyas, is $35 and can be ordered through The National Women's Law Center, 1616 P Street NW, Suite 100, Washington, D.C. 20036. Phone: (202) 328-5160

Playing Fair: A Guide to Title IX in High School and College Sports, by Kathryn M. Reith, can be ordered through The Women's Sports Foundation, Eisenhower Park, East Meadow, NY 11554. Phone 1-800-227-3988 or (516) 542-4700

The Equity in Athletics Disclosure Act

This act went into effect in October of 1996 as part of the Improving America's Schools Act of 1994, and it states that all institutions of higher education which have intercollegiate athletic programs and which receive any federal funds are required to complete annual reports with information concerning gender equity in their intercollegiate athletic programs. The act was created to make prospective students and student-athletes aware of the commitment a particular institution has made to ensure equal athletic opportunities for its male and female students. The report must be made available by the school to students, prospective students, parents, or interested persons who request it no later than October 15 of each year. The report must include the following information pertaining to the particular institution:

1. The number of male and female full-time undergraduates attending the institution
2. A listing of the varsity teams that are involved in intercollegiate athletic competition, and:
   a. The total number of team members
   b. The total operating expenses (such as money spent on lodging and meals, transportation, staff salaries, uniforms, and equipment) for each team
   c. Whether the head coach is male or female, and whether that coach is full-time or part-time. The number of assistant coaches who are male and female for each team, and whether they are full-time or part-time
3. The total amount of money spent on athletic scholarships for men and the amount spent on athletic scholarships for women
4. The total amount of money spent on recruiting, reported separately for men's and women's teams

5. The total amount of revenue generated by all-men's teams and the amount generated by all-women's teams

6. The average annual salary of the head coach of the men's teams, and the average annual salary of the head coach of the women's team

(See page 206 for more information about requesting these reports from colleges.)

The Student Right-to-Know and Campus Security Act of 1990

This law requires that colleges and universities which receive federal funds release their security policies and the three most recent years of campus crime statistics to prospective students upon request. This published information should include statistics for murder, sex offenses (forcible and non-forcible), robbery, aggravated assault, burglary, and motor-vehicle theft. The report should also provide arrest statistics relating to liquor-law violations, drug-abuse violations, and weapons possessions.

(See page 204 for more information about requesting crime reports from colleges.)

other resources

The following are organizations, Web sites, and other resources you can use to help with your college search. Many
public libraries now offer free Internet access.

Liberal-Arts Colleges

Liberal Arts College Web site
http://www.liberalarts.org/
   Contains links to many liberal-arts colleges' Web sites,
and information about a liberal-arts education.

Consortium of Liberal Arts Colleges on the World Wide
Web
http://www.wabash.edu/clac
   Has links to over fifty liberal-arts colleges' home pages.

Private Colleges and Universities

The Independent Higher Education Network
http://www.fihe.org
   Has links to 630 private college and universities, and
financial-aid information for private colleges.

General College Information

Yahoo! Search
http://www.yahoo.com/regional/countries/United_States/Education/Colleges_and_Universities
   This search through Yahoo! will help you find college sites.

Campus Newspapers

College Press Network
http://www.cpnet.com/
   Has links to hundreds of on-line campus newspapers.

Women's Colleges

The Women's College Coalition
   Promotes and publicizes the value of women's colleges. To receive information about women's colleges, contact The Women's College Coalition, 125 Michigan Avenue NE, Washington, D.C. 20017; (202) 234-0443.

Success at a Women's College
http://home.judson.edu/why.html
   Contains statistics about women's colleges and women's college graduates.

The Women's College Link Page
http://tln.lib.mi.us/~lptotter/
   Has links to women's colleges arranged by state and religious affiliation, and whether two-year or four-year degrees are offered.

Black Colleges

Gateway to Historically Black Colleges and Universities Internet Servers

http://www.eng.ncat.edu/hbcu.html

Provides a list of the nation's Historically Black Colleges and Universities (HBCU), as well as links to many HBCU home pages.

Community Colleges

The Community College Web

http://www.mcli.dist.maricopa.edu/cc/

Has links to over 500 community colleges' Web pages, and information about community-college education.

Religious Colleges

Member Listing of the Coalition for Christian Colleges and Universities

http://www1.gospelcom.net/cgi–bin/cccu_alpha

Offers links to many of the nation's Christian colleges and universities.

AJCUnet

http://www.ajcunet.edu/

The Web site of the Association of Jesuit Colleges and Universities, it offers links to many of these schools.

Military

How the Military Will Help You Pay for College: The complete source of information on the Military's billion-dollar tuition support programs by Don Betterton

Describes military programs and military-related financial-aid programs. As well as explaining each of the nation's military programs, it provides information for women considering military academies or ROTC, and the specific requirements for female service members. To order, contact Peterson's Guides at 1-800-338-3282.

Students of Color

The Higher Education Moneybook for Minorities and Women by William C. Young

A listing of scholarships for students of color and for women, arranged by field of interest (such as education, English, computer science, history). It is $23 and can be ordered from The Higher Education Moneybook, Young Enterprises Int'l, 5937 16th Street NW, Washington, D.C. 20011; (202) 829-0039.

Directory of Financial Aids for Minorities 1995–1997 by Gail Ann Schlachter and R. David Weber

A directory of information about more than 2,000 scholarships, fellowships, grants, loans, awards, and internships just for students of color. With the book costing $47.50 a copy, you may want to ask your high school guidance center to order it for the department. To order it for yourself, send check to Reference Service Press, 1100 Industrial Road, Suite 9, San Carlos, CA 94070; (415) 594-0743.

Black Excel: The College Help Network
http://cnct.com/home/ijblack/BlackExcel.shtml

A college admissions and scholarship service for African-American students. It contains a listing of over 350 scholarships.

MOLIS

http://web.fie.com/web/mol/index.htm

Provides information about historically black colleges and universities and Hispanic-serving institutions. It also has information about scholarships.

Lesbian, Gay, and Bisexual Students

Infoqueer

http://www.infoqueer.org/queer/qis/college.html

Provides links to lesbian, gay, and bisexual student organizations' home pages at many colleges and universities.

Students with Disabilities

Financial Aid for the Disabled and Their Families 1996–1998 by Gail Ann Schlachter and R. David Weber

Contains 900 funding programs for students with disabilities and children of parents with disabilities. It is $39.50 and can be ordered from Reference Service Press, 1100 Industrial Road, Suite 9, San Carlos, CA 94070; (415) 594-0743.

Sports

The Women's Sports Foundation College Athletic Scholarship Guide

A listing of the colleges and universities that offer athletic scholarships for women. Each entry includes the name and address of the school, tuition costs, enrollment numbers, sports offered, whether scholarships are full or partial, and the number of scholarships available. It is $3 from The Women's Sports Foundation, Eisenhower Park, East Meadow, NY 11554; 1-800-227-3988.

Guide for the College-Bound Student-Athlete

The NCAA free guide for college-bound student-athletes has information about academic eligibility, financial aid, recruiting, and much more. Order from National Collegiate Athletic Association (NCAA), 6201 College Blvd., Overland Park, KS 66211-2422; 1-800-638-3731.

Gender Equity in Sports
http://www.arcade.uiowa.edu/proj/ge/

Offers information about gender equity in collegiate sports, up-to-date news on Title IX related complaints and lawsuits, as well as reports on colleges which are under Title IX review.

Women's Studies

The Artemis Guide to Women's Studies Programs throughout the United States
http://www.users.interport.net/~kater/

Contains links to many colleges' women's-studies department home pages.

Women's Studies Programs
http://www-unix.umbc.edu/~korenman/wmst/programs.html

Has links to many women's-studies department home pages.

Crime

Academic Crime Statistics Link Guide
http://www.crime.org/links__academic.html

Has links to many college security-department home

pages, which have postings of up-to-date campus-crime reports.

Security on Campus
http://www.soconline.org
Contains campus-crime statistics, legislative information relating to campus crime, and the organization's newsletter *Crime Watch*, which includes crime reports from colleges across the country. You can also contact Security on Campus at 215 West Church Road, Suite 200, King of Prussia, PA 19406-3207; (610) 768-9330.

Dorm Life

Residential Life and Housing Home Pages
http://www.whitman.edu/~hedgesaj/stuaff/housing.html
A fun site which has links to many college dorms.

Greek Sites

Greek Pages
http://www.greekpages.com/docs/search.html
Links you to sorority and fraternity chapters' home pages at over 500 schools.

Greek Home Pages
http://web.mit.edu/afs/athena.mit.edu/activity/i/ifc/www/grschool.html
Has links to many sorority and fraternity chapters' home pages at colleges across the country.

Financial Aid

The U.S. Department of Education's Federal Financial Aid Information Hotline: 1-800-433-3243 (1-800-4-FED-AID)

This service is available 8 a.m. to 8 p.m. EST. Upon request you can receive free *The Student Guide* (listed below) and Free Application for Federal Student Aid (FAFSA). They also answer general financial-aid questions, help with the filing of your application, tell you whether a school participates in federal student-aid programs, and explain federal student eligibility requirements.

The Student Guide (1996–97)—Financial Aid from the U.S. Department of Education

Published free by the U.S. Department of Education, it provides comprehensive information about federal financial aid. A must for anyone planning to apply for financial aid. Order from The Federal Student Aid Information Center, P.O. Box 84, Washington, D.C. 20044 or call 1-800-433-3243. Updated yearly.

The 1995–1997 edition of the *Directory of Financial Aids for Women*

Contains more than 1,500 listings of funding opportunities specifically for women for study, research, travel, training, career development, and innovative effort. Scholarships, fellowships, grants, loans, awards, and internships are included. Entries contain information about the program, sponsoring organization, telephone number, fax and E-mail addresses, purpose, eligibility, remuneration, duration, special features, limitations, number of awards, and deadline dates. Written by Gail Ann Schlachter, the 498-page book costs $45 plus $4 for shipping. It is the most thorough women's financial-aid resource available. You may want to ask your high school guidance center to order it for the department. Many public libraries also have it in their reference or college section. To order it for yourself, send check to Reference Service Press, 1100 Industrial Road, Suite 9, San Carlos, CA 94070; or call (415) 594-0743.

Dollars for College: The Quick Guide to Financial Aid for Women in All Fields

The approximately 90-page booklet contains sections on federal-aid programs, financial-aid terminology, and a numbered list of 349 briefly described financial-aid programs aimed at women students. Includes an index that locates information by field, state, and special groupings, such as re-entry women, sorority members, and women's colleges. Available for $6.95 from Garrett Park Press, P.O. Box 190D, Garrett Park, MD 20896; or (301) 946-2553. Booklet is revised every twelve to eighteen months.

The Higher Education Moneybook for Minorities and Women, by William C. Young

Lists scholarships for students of color and women, arranged by field of interest (such as education, English, computer science, history). It is $23. Contact The Higher Education Moneybook, Young Enterprises Int'l, 5937 16th Street NW, Washington, D.C. 20011; (202) 829-0039 or 800-516-9960.

Barron's Complete College Financing Guide, 1995

Offers basic information about financial aid, with a chapter on scholarships and awards for women (many of which are for women already in college). It is a great resource for finding financial aid throughout college. It is $14.95. Contact Barron's Education Series, Inc., Hauppage, NY; (516) 434-3311.

The Women's Sports Foundation College Athletic Scholarship Guide

A state-by-state guide to colleges and universities offering athletic scholarships to women. Each entry includes the name and address of the school, tuition costs, enrollment numbers, sports offered, whether scholarships are full or partial, and the number of scholarships available. It is $3 from The Women's Sports Foundation, Eisenhower Park, East Meadow, NY 11554; 1-800-227-3988.

Project EASI—Easy Access for Students and Institutions
http://easi.ed.gov

Initiated by the Department of Education to provide students with information from federal and state governments, individual institutions, and private sources on topics such as financial aid, admissions testing, and student loans.

Money Matters
http://www.ed.gov/money.html

Created by the Department of Education. Contains information about financial aid and news about higher education. This site allows users to complete and submit the Free Application for Federal Student Aid (FAFSA) on-line.

The Financial Aid Information Page
http://www.finaid.org/

Offers a lot of financial-aid information, including sources of aid just for women.

Standardized Tests

Test Score Optional Colleges

For an up-to-date list of colleges which do not require students to submit SAT and/or ACT scores, send a self-addressed, stamped envelope to Test Score Optional List, FairTest, 342 Broadway, Cambridge, MA 02139.

ACT

For information about the ACT, and to receive a free booklet called *Preparing for the ACT*, contact the ACT offices at (319) 337-1270.

The following sites provide students with information about the SAT, test dates, and a way to register for the test on-line.

The Educational Testing Service Network
http://www.ets.org/body.html

College Board Online
http://www.collegeboard.org/

Applying On-line

Peterson's Application Center
http://www.petersons.com/apply.html
Allows you to fill out and submit applications electronically for over 200 institutions.

Organizations Supporting Women in Higher Education

Women in Higher Education
http://www.wihe.com
Contains information regarding issues for women in college.

American Association of University Women
http://www.aauw.org/
Contains information about gender equity in education.

acknowledgments

I thank my parents, Ellen and John Page, for going into retirement only to have new full-time jobs fielding my phone calls regarding this book.

It has been a joy to have Elisabeth Kallick Dyssegaard as my editor. She has made this book and this year everything I wanted it to be. Denise Oswald's ideas have helped shape this book, too, and I am grateful to have had her insight.

Fate visited me both at a cocktail party and over the phone in the forms of Ron Lieber and Anthony Tedesco. I thank them for getting the ball rolling.

I thank Liz Maguire and Karen Wolny for being role models, surrogate agents, and protectors when I say the wrong thing at a dinner party; James Alonso, Lucia Bowes, Anita Colley, Jeremy Krane, and Ilan Sandberg for making college everything my parents hoped it wouldn't be (special added thanks to Ilan for being the patron saint of designated drivers and to Anita for donating her wealth of wit to parts of this book); my professors at Goucher for making college everything I hoped it would be; my able assistant, Bella Vie; my agent, Neeti Madan; Deborah Kirk and Mark Schapiro for recommending young, talented writers; Katherine Davis VanLaw for her constructive critique and encouragement; the Fishmans and Davises for their support (especially David

Fishman for technical support); the women at *Ms.* magazine for creating my inspiration for this book; and all the writers for their blind faith, generosity, and brilliance.

I thank the following women for taking time out of their busy college lives to help with this book and for sharing their experiences and perspectives with me: Shira Adler, Rhonda Allen, Christina Allick, Margie Alsbrook, Kristin Anderson, Kate Barber, Shannon Barry, Kimberly Bartman, Lori Baughman, Julie Beam, Jessica Benjamin, Nancy Benson-Nicol, Julie Berman, Jennifer Bhatia, Lise Bohn, Alison Bozzi, Apryl Bragg, Niko Bronson, Stephanie Brown, Phyllis Browne, Jean Burdett, Becky Cary, Beth Cashara, Karmelle Chaise, Melanie Chapin, Susan Chenelle, Rachel Cohen, Dorey Cole, Paulette Cook, Cecilia Cygnar, Christine Dias, Laura Didyk, Kristen Druffner, Dawn Dungan, Valerie Dunn, Noelle Everett, Christina Finzel, Jessica Fisher, Amanda Geerts, Jennifer Greene, Alison Grizzle, Laurell Haapanen, Ann Hake, Anne Halsey, Rachel Heacock, Tanya Hedges, Julia Heemstra, Inga Herrmann, Holly Hillard, Susanna Hines, Leslie Holland, Amanda Howland, Kristen Hubbard, Amy Hufft, Marcie Hume, Yumna Jafri, Laudan Jahromi, Rana Jaleel, Megan Johnson, Ghillian Keefe, Jessica Knauss, Kristine Kupfer, Jennifer Lacher, Jessamyn Larrabee, Susan Levison, Amber Lewis, Alison Liles, Christine McBride, Kimberly McBride, Sloan McMullin, Leslie Madsen, Laura Malone, Ensa Matthews, Christina Maxwell, Christine Medeiros, Amy Meredith, Hillary Meyer, Dana Kristen Miller, Elizabeth Monagan, Amy Morrison, Karen Morrissey, Jessica Mueller, Eustacia Muir, Lisa Murphy, Judy Nallella, Janna Nielsen, Kim O'Neal, Melissa Ozawa, Martha Palazij, Kristi Park, Rebecca Parks, Sarah Pederson, Meredith Phebus, Catholyn Pickup, Megan Pruiett, Meghan Reedy, Elizabeth Revard, Lindy Robinett,

Rebecca Belle Robinson, Jackie Sadker, Sarah Scheckter, Evalina Schmuckler, Clarissa Schoenhals, Claire Schomp, Melissa Schultz, Carrie Sendrow, Emily Shavers, Kelley Sheehan, Suzanne Shelly, Jodi Sherman, Jill Sink, Charlotte Spears, Christine St. John, Anne Stoltenberg, Jessica Stutman, Margreta Sundelin, Shinobu Tateuchi, Mandana Towfiq, Andreya Valabek, Yvette Vallejera, Jeanine Van Norman, Hannah Van Sickle, Laura Warren, Cynthia Waters, Tracey Watts, Dawn-Marie Webster, Kim Whipple, Rachel Widome, Ayanna William, Lynn Wingert, and Sarah Wohlford.

I thank the following professors, graduate assistants, and coaches for their enthusiasm in promoting young talent. Without them this book would not be. Ralph Adamo, Loyola New Orleans; Rebecca Albert, Temple; Scott Allen, United States Naval Academy; Nathalie Anderson, Swarthmore; George Barlow, Grinnell; Richard Barnes, Pomona; Eric Benjamin, U. of the South; Ann Marie Bentson, Western Piedmont Community College; Kim Bridgford, Fairfield; Susan Carpenter, Antioch; Nancy Chinn, Baylor; Janice Christianson, South Dakota State; Kenneth Cook, Prescott; Bland Crowder, Hendrix; Charles Crupi, Albion; Mike D'Aquino, West Point; Mary Margaret Fanno, Ohio State; Stephen Finley, Haverford; Peter Gale-Nelson, Brown; Claude Gibson, Texas A&M; Judy Gill, Dickinson; Dr. Gooding, Oakwood; Judith Goodwin, Grand View; Gail Griffin, Kalamazoo; Linda Hagge, Iowa State; Wayne Hoffman-Ogier, Bennington; Cynthia Huntington, Dartmouth; Suzanne Jones, U. of Richmond; Michael Keenan, Macalester; Gillian Kendall, Birmingham Southern U.; Michael Klein, U. of Arkansas; Greg Lanier, U. of West Florida; Nancy Leonard, Bard; Richard Lemp, United States Air Force Academy; Suzanne Marrs, Millsaps; Thomas Mauch,

Colorado College; Russell Meyer, Emporia State; Kristen Miller, Oakland City U.; Dr. Nicols, U. of Pittsburgh; William Nicols, Denison; Dr. Novak, Pepperdine; Elizabeth Perry, Sarah Lawrence; Ann Peyton, Florida Atlantic U.; Mary Pinard, Babson; Albert Rivero, Marquette; Randa Ryan, U. of Texas-Austin; Jean Sanborn, Colby; Constantine Santas, Flagler; Debra Schaffer, Montana State; Natalia Singer, St. Lawrence; Barbara Smith, Alderson-Broaddus; Sue Standing, Wheaton; Jackie Sweeney, Ulster County Community College; Deborah Tall, Hobart & William Smith; Pat Wagner, Tompkins Cortland Community College; Scott Ward, Eckerd; and Diane Wendt, U. of Denver. I'd like especially to thank Mary Kay Baron, U. of North Florida; Madison Smartt Bell, Goucher; Jane Brickman, United States Merchant Marine Academy; Jean Carwile-Masteller, Whitman; Nancy Coveney, U. of Kentucky; Neil Daniel, Texas Christian; Elizabeth Dodd, Kansas State; Sarah Goodwin, Skidmore; Gail Griffin, Kalamazoo; Katherine Linehan, Oberlin; Kim McMullen, Kenyon; Christopher Merrill, Holy Cross; Jeff Nunokawa, Princeton; Diane Raptosh, Albertson; Eve Schulnet, Holy Cross; and Marcia Smeltzer, Colorado State.

I would also like to thank Bob Schaeffer of FairTest, April Osajima of the American Association of University Women, and Ellen Wilkins of Safe Campuses Now for their help and for being such wonderful advocates of women's and girls' rights in education.